WHEELSONG POETRY ANTHOLOGY

Edited by

Steve Wheeler
Charlene Phare
Brandon Adam Haven

First published by
Wheelsong Books
4 Willow Close,
Plymouth PL3 6EY,
United Kingdom

First published in 2022

Print ISBN: 979-8-84753-153-5

"Poetry is when an emotion has found its thought and the thought has found words."

– Robert Frost

FUNDRAISING IN AID OF

Save the Children

Contents

Foreword

Welcome to the first Wheelsong poetry anthology and thank you for purchasing a copy of this wonderful collection.

As with previous anthologies published by Wheelsong Books, all the proceeds from Amazon sales will be donated to Save the Children, a global relief fund for children in crisis. From the past sales of anthologies we have been able to help fund a camel library for unschooled children in Ethiopia and urgent relief for the youngest refugees of the Ukraine war.

93 poets from several Facebook poetry groups have kindly donated 183 poems to help raise funds. The poetry is eclectic, covering many themes and is presented in many different styles. All the poems were subject to a rigorous peer review process, where the identities of the writers were unknown to the editorial board.

Between us, Charlene, Brandon and I have selected what we hope is a representative sample of the wonderful talents found in all our poetry groups. We would like to thank the admin and members of Wheelsong Poetry Group, Soulful Poetry, Poet's Corner, Pure Poetry, Safe Haven and Poetry UK for generously supporting this venture.

As you enjoy reading through this book, you can be assured that purchasing it is really making a difference to a child somewhere in the world.

Steve Wheeler
CEO Wheelsong Books
October 2022

Duet

By Carmen Megiddo

Quietly, the darkness drifts upon the air,
Snatched softly from beneath a sluggish sea,
The withered vine awaits for you and me
In final rending of a solitary tear

Lightning frames your voice within the night,
Before it grows into the yellowed leaf
Without my audience, this pain and grief
Blooms into verses of your wild delight.

Laying bound and gagged within your lies
I sang a song of freedom faithfully
And there it searched my soul to bring the key
Gathered to greet me with a calm eye.

Buttered Berried

By Janetta Lamourt

I loved my Aunt Fran,
her homemade buttered scones,
and blueberry jam. Blue ribbon winning
blueberry jam she would remind me
and point out the ribbons
she carefully pinned to the wall and I
nodded in agreement—licking butter berried
sticky fingers. She sat in the kitchen with me,
teapot fresh off the hob, apron laces
stretched around a comforting hug of a waist
I could not reach my arms
around… because freshly buttered scones
and blueberry jam were favourites too.

Face of the Moon

By Rafik Romdhani

The face of the moon is the last thing
a pigeon sees on its own slaughter
by the dark while dancing with its wound
in the hands of death.
Blood oozing, covering the stem of a rose
like a red cloud resembling nothing,
dripping from the eye of a wolf irked
by distance and by the ice of despair.
The face of the moon is dark's puzzle
flickering between the past and the present
like a sacrifice above the worries of the wind,
a golden tear for the thirst of a dream,
a breast cut from Aphrodite's soul
and cast like a shrapnel to kill dogmas
in cold hearts and free minds' magmas.
The face of the moon is the sun's innocence
of infancy after its disappearance behind time
and space's recondite back.
We won't have the same shadows
and destinations here under the moon.
Our screams will be heard now.
The call of the waves will reach mountains'
ears more clearly, and the hands of death
will be more merciful at the bottom
of this luminous chalice hanging from
the invisible throne of God.
The last thing dust sees before it is imprisoned
in dew drops is the face of the moon,
before it weaves the long threads of absence.
How cruel and tormenting is absence.
The face of the moon: the last piece of cheese
a crow in vain opens its mouth for, and flies across.
The last thing a pigeon sees
on its own slaughter by the dark while dancing
with its wound in the hands of death
is of course the face of the moon.

Fallen King

By Jon Wright

No crown upon my head
No sceptre in my hand
Noose of gold on my neck
On the edge I stand
Kingdom of rubble
Throne broken glass
Hope shattered
Watching time pass
Step from the edge
With a drop and a snap
Dance the last dance
Hung by my mind's trap
The crown may fall
The throne may burn
Riches are worthless
If the king does not return
Don't be the fallen king
Reach out and talk
Kingdoms can rebuild
Don't let this be your last walk

Awaken

By Brandon Adam Haven

Awaken from golden slumber and dreams entailed,
I recognize the beauty of life as I grow more frail
Brightness again enters into my deteriorating room
As I rise up with hope in my heart to battle the gloom
Haunted by memories lost in the dark recesses of time
I loathe rise and glow in such a glimmering shine
Love and hope, chisel away the stone of my heart
To many tears lately I've shed, now to joyfully embark

Ripples

By Tom Cleary

The iambic feet of time
rhythmically lull us into
tenuously tied cradles
hung from treetops
whose very lives depend on
ever expanding rings
much as the ripples in a pond
until our lives, cut down and hewn
transform to boxes
into which others store us
as memories
for even waves reach a shore.

The Weather Vane

By Adam Whitworth

Peppering the rural landscape
like worn gargoyles on churches
like found horseshoes nailed to the nearest plank
How many of these weather-vanes actually work?
This one, set in its ways
gives evidence for the unmoved.
The blacksmith fell deeply in love
with the ornamental, the old peculiar
village ways and impenetrable mysteries.
The blacksmith's ingenuity
is spun from the earliest forge.
The blacksmith, long gone, has left
a worthy memorial. Permanently
pointing North-West, as good
a direction as any.
This weather-vane works well
in its adherence to beauty
easy harmony and rising wonder.

Paris in the Rain

By Steve Wheeler

Two nights in Paris had me feeling stoked
But soon I was examining my scars
I'm getting colder and my feet are soaked
and I've been splashed by several cars

The clouds are heavy and the sky turns black
This deluge is persistent, zut alors!
It hits the pavement then it bounces back
No, it never rains in Paris, but it pours

The narrow roads run like a mountain stream
Precipitation pouring from a broken dam
and me caught out without my overcoat,
huddled in a doorway of the Bataclan

Dodging round the puddles in the taxi ranks
La pluie de printemps tombe toujours
Far from the shadow of la Tour Eiffel
No, it never rains in Paris, but it pours

Queening

By Jannetta Lamourt

The king hides
while the queen
sallies forth to do battle.
The knight gambols
while the bishop works his angles
left to right or was it right to left?
The pawn steps forward one square at a time
across the battlefield of black and white.
But I wonder if the pawn,
once it reaches its destination
Transforms into the blood-thirsty battler
or quails—a pawn in queen's clothing.

Hope Alive

By Lawal Ibrahim Hibie

We have burnt yesterdays
Into a ton of histories,
We let every moment fade into the airways
And boxed the leftover ashes into our memories.

We could remember the kids we were as teens
The juvenile delinquents we played
And how all stars were counted on the sea.
Better days have far gone when we couldn't see
The beauty of time and nature that laid,
How we wish we were keen!

How we hope we were sane enough
To build bridge than wall
But we put ego at the middle of our circle
We kept malice hanging between our ribs
We fought forth and back—to our cribs
Leaving life stranded in the death's manacle
We strove to thrive tall
We forget that "Life lives where there is love."

We came but never saw in the hood
How the red river bounded us as humanity.
Had we known "There is no good, other than doing good"
We could have let love lead this vicinity

But today, we count on many days afflicted with furious
Days, when written on the cloud many stories
Indelible enough as they were washed off by the bays;
Hoping ahead and alive for recherché days.

Fire in Her Eyes

By Kenneth Drysdale

I've felt the icy shadows
Crawling through her dreams
She reached out for my hand
So I could see the streams
Frozen shards floating in strands
Chained garden formerly gleams
Scattered pieced petals of her flowers
Did you see the fire in her eyes?
A lioness roars out her power
In the field of fears echoing with cries
Did you see the fire in her eyes?
I'll never forget that crystal sight
When I saw sapphire flames
Swirling within those glossy spheres
I'll never be the same
After she consumed my fears
Resting in my heart she claims
It was always part of her regime
Did you see the fire in her eyes?
She can leap bounds in all extremes
Along the horizon she bends sunrise
Did you see the fire in her eyes?
I'm mesmerized upon blazing shores
Purifying blue holding the ashes
Caressed ambience, flickering lights
Eternal beauty of internal splashes
Melting the core without a fight
Concentrated within bolts of their flashes
Explosive desires dance of a frigid land
Did you see the fire in her eyes?
She reached out for my hand
Burning so free up high in the skies
Did you see the fire in her eyes?

A Voice Like His

By Autumn Burniston

I've heard organ voices
That could rumble through marble floors—
I've heard southern honey like you've never heard before—
And I've heard leather voices, voices like creaky stairs—
I've heard voices like a slapping wind,
and voices like chalk on chairs

But only once I've ever heard, a voice like his, and he
Sounds like kaleidoscope beads
in a tin can sea.

I've heard voices like sliding wood on wood,
Voices like running streams,
I've heard the likes of purrs and sirens come out of human beings,
I've heard wind chimes, and clinking dimes
I've heard flits about a room,
Avalanches—small then crashing down on all ears they might consume

But only once I've ever heard, a voice like his , and he
Sounds like kaleidoscope beads
in a tin can sea

I'm listening for some change of shape
I'm looking for the coloured rain
I'm feeling for that middle range rumble
That if you've never heard you can't explain

Because only once I've ever heard, a voice like his and he,
Sounds like kaleidoscope beads in a tin can sea

Yearning at the Yale

By Autumn Burniston

I saw them in the window
And I've wanted ever since
To dance with somebody I love
But I'm still learning patience
And when life is slow
I want to dance with somebody I love

And where there is music
Late into the night
The older couple sways
Slow step to the right
And I clumsily move just to watch them

And then the pretty eyed girl
With her rainbow chance boy
Dance both so full of love
They swing and they turn
Like two kids in a park with
Hours to burn in their love

I get starry-eyed,
My soul is on fire
And I want to dance with the man that I love
But I watch them from the side
As they wiggle and glide
and they move how they know how to love

With each last leg of a tune
That thunders the room,
I see the dancers in the kitchen in love
In faces of strangers on bar floors
Clink glasses, voices all raw over love

Then I sit at a table
And for as long as I'm able
I try to freeze-frame the feelings of love
A sweet souvenir
Of another night near,
And another prayer closer to love

Promise You'll Be Here

By Allen Baswell

Promise you'll be here…
To take away all my pain
And to let me love again
Promise you'll be here and will be mine
To let my inner love light shine
Promise me you won't play games with my heart
And that we will never grow apart
Promise you'll be here – to be everything to me
To love and cherish one another for all eternity
Not to be a fantasy…but a forever reality

Dandy Highwayman

By Rhiannon Owens

Woodpecker imposter
Poor man's Kingfisher,
An upside down Dick Turpin
Eyes all a-glitter,

Careful, inquisitive
You scan all around,
There are nuts to be had
You flit to the ground,

The seeds are good too
Your talons grasp the mesh,
Your slim beak so strong
As you dig and you peck,

This furtive visitor
Mysterious masked stranger,
Head always cocked
Alert to all danger!

Silence

By Jon Wright

Drifting like a feather on the breeze
Fluttering down like snow
The silence almost too much to bear
Which way to turn, which way to go
To hear a sound like thunder
Would scare me to my core
But to hear only silence
Would break me so much more
To never hear the song of the morning
Or even the dance of rain
To never hear those I love
Would be like a world of pain
Never to hear a babies cry
Never to hear the choirs song
Never to hear the music of my heart
Never to know where I belong
The silence as loud as a cry from the heavens
A rumble of nothingness fills the air
Silence of my heart, silence of my soul
Silence all around me, not a sound from the fair
As I walk the silent road
To the door of my silent home
Close the door behind me
And sit on my silent throne

If You See Her

By John Rennie

I know plenty of people
Don't say much more than "Hello,
Hi, how are you?" It's so idle
And everybody knows
I could have said so much more
But she wouldn't have heard me anyway
On the darkest night I found the door

To another life and went so astray
Blood Moon, under the one grey cloud
Reddish drizzle soaked my mind
And soon, thunder pounded so loud
Lightning briefly ghosted me in kind

"If you see her, say hello,"
Was playing in the car
If you see her, let her know
I never meant her any harm

There was a difference of opinion
So we just went our separate ways
It could have been different, still I
Realised I couldn't have stayed
So much can be gleaned from one's eyes
I know what they mean about windows and souls
As I look up into the misty skies
All I can see are limited highs and lows
I could have done so much better
I never really tried all that hard
I should have at least let her
Know that she helped me from the start

"If you see her, say hello,"
Is still playing in the car
When you see her, let her know
I never meant her any harm

I'll just keep on moving on
But always with my ears to the ground
I hear so many comments and
They're just echoes of her sound
Blood Moon, on a brooding night
We never got to say goodbye
I just upped and then took flight
Couldn't stay to explain why
She sees plenty of people
Who take up most of her time
I know that the reason

Was an inexcusable crime
Everything will always change
Inevitably, also, you and me
"Nothing can't remain the same,"
He said, so mysteriously

"If you see her, say hello,"
Forever playing in my car
When you see her, let her know
That I wrote this song for her.

A Beach Somewhere

By Patrik Jonez

Cool-whip clouds wafting,
Lazy gauze soft'ning
a sea of sapphire glitter,
Poseidon's hither,

Bluest hues, newest muse,
Sprawling against the horizon,
Diffused, amused by the shipping breeze,
Seagulls dive and weave
in tumbling threes, breath-taking bumble sprees,
Pleased, grinning children pay toothy homage,
pointing, anointing them court gestures,

Salty sandcastles tassel the shore,
rapport with foamy kissing tides,
Rinsing nights, of lover's footprints,
Hence, the moon poses as the sun,
Warm with a silver glow,
An eye of snow,
In the face of God's artistry

Unfair

By Brian Keith

Can you tell me a story
That I have not heard before
The butcher, the baker
They are truly such a bore

Can you write me a note
That gives me a clue
But follows a new path
To find out that it's you

Can you show me a murder
That cannot be solved
And end the long story
Unsure of who was involved

Can you guide me along
A dark twisted path
That leads to a clearing
Too late to see the stash

Can there be no plot
Or strange happenings
Or find that the bad guy
Had gotten away with everything

I'm sure you can
But what would it be
That draws in the reader
In such a mystery

I'll end this with a warning
To those not aware
That endings can be unhappy
And completely unfair

The Face of Time

By Yanny Widjanarko

Tick, tock, tick, tock...
(Echoing)
Unrealistic gears move in a slow gesture
While each wheel slips inter dimensions in durations
Sketching the face of time
Knitting the wool of momentum
Dimension overlaps by numbers
Mysteries trapped at the gap of hollow
Remained as shadow, swallowed
At the core of anecdote, restless
The face of time is the stiches of fate
The figure created by the long of continuum
Once it's completed, the eyes of the truth reveal
From a cryptical room quietly blooms
Flowers are the pain enlightened in red
As blushing as the wounds were there
The visage of abstractions has sealed
Find the meaning, in these interludes of exudes.

Rained Off

By Neil Mason

Eagerly awaiting the test match radio commentary
Prepared my cheese and tomato sandwiches
into oval shapes
The radio crackled, appearing to clear its throat
As it had been playing too much music lately
I gave it some tunes to make it feel better
Storm clouds raced in from the pavilion end
with the aggression of a fast bowler
Tear stumps fell to the ground crying on sticky wickets
Waterlogged umpire raised his finger signalling
the test match was rained off
I was stumped, what could I do now?
I tried to finish the daily paper crossword
But I was too angry

Phoenix Rising

By Antonella Caiazza

Dare to be free.
Dare to make sense.
Live authentically.
Feel,
Be intense.
Defy all the odds;
Defy and descend.

Survive;
No, thrive,
Despite their dissent.
Into the darkness,
Into the war,
A lightning bolt
of truth
to ignore.

The sounds of their whispers,
The sound of your roar,
Evolving,
Revolving,
This ever-raging door.
Reason and ration,
all just a game.

Pawns used as prizes
to loudly proclaim.
And yet,
rise above,
Fan all the flames.
With new wings of glory,
Fly once again.

When I Bleed

By Abril Garcia Linn

When I bleed I remember you
Under fire red sky
You were meant to die
You never made it past the first 2 months
I almost didn't know you existed
Until I felt you leave
Warm milk between my legs
Invisible hot poker stabbing my womb
Twisting me into knots
You weren't ready for us
We weren't ready for you
Although your brief existence was a secret
I still mourn you

fallen

By John Thornton

i am falling
falling so far
nothing to stop me
my minds where you are
can i leave
leave you alone
it's very chilling
i am chilled to the bone
now i have fallen
fallen too far
no one to help me
can't see where you are
how does this happen
happens so fast
trapped in this madness
no future no past

My Love

By Kenneth Wheeler

When I no longer see your vision
In the pages of my mind, or recall
The happy sounds of laughter
Within my dreams I find.

When I no longer hear your sweet
Voice, echoing down the avenues
Of time, that is vibrating new life
Within this aching heart of mine.

When I don't feel the sense of
Your presence during busy days,
I deeply regret every moment
Apart, until my quietness I regain.

I have this deep desire to spend
Each moment of every day within
Your presence, for true love will
Always remain, it never goes away.

Within the cavities of my heart,
The everlasting desire I crave is
Secreted within my soul, patiently
Awaiting the breaking of the day.

After the Rain

By Sema Okoko

The front of the house has a warm glow
And the grasses are still stained with dew.
Standing beside the old bucket
and worn-out rake,
I lean my hands on the rusty rail and
Try to enjoy the view after the rain

Taken But Never Lost
By Jon Wright

Like wilted flowers in the ground
Like the birds made no sound
The voices of those taken too soon
Like the sun eclipsed by the moon
No longer the clock ticks in time
No more their poem will rhyme
Gone before their painting was complete
Never again in life we would meet
Memories are all we have to hold
To make sure their stories are told
Taken by such horrible illness
Their world filled with a stillness
They may be taken, but never lost
Melted away like early morning frost
But the sun with never take them from our mind
In there you will always find
Their smiling faces, their warm embrace
Always there in your happy place
To hold your hand when you miss them so
When in your heart they will never go
Like a flower blooming in the morning light
Like beautiful birds that take flight
Memories of them have no cost
They may be taken, but never lost

A Swing in Tandem
By Melanie Garfinkle Waknine

Wooden horizontal and vertical
supporting all but the spiritual.
Emotional quiet, hop-scotches around
a swing in time devoid of sound.
Rustic planks weathered by tears
offer unguided confidence understood by fears.
A limitless euphoric swinging up on high

an intense low- swaying back to
Deny, to defy...
Heartache
Heartbreak
Love on the swing
a melodic, poetic oscillating fling!
Forged flow of feelings to and fro
humbling, yet asserting
remaining in tow...

The Soul's Rhapsody

By Rafik Romdhani

Oh poetry, take me back to father's shadow
while he reads fate on the face of clouds,
and fathoms life with his seasoned eyes,
while he smells petrichor approaching
fast like a healer for the ills in men
and in the air reminiscent of freedom.
Take me back to myself, to my soft pillow
under which I hide my new shoes
that I from time to time wake up to try.
Return me to me the way my father's hand
returns wheat to the ground with soul's rhapsody,
and broad sweeps
before at any moment rain hits us,
before hungry birds and ants devour
the seeds of creation inside my ribs.
Oh ink, carry me to my bare feet,
to the antique olive oil jar
which offers me a selfie, gives me back
my face, my hair, and my mouth's vapour
whenever I stare into it.
Carry me back, haemorrhage
to that leaking ceiling which imprisons
the invisible breasts of the azure
and squeezes the patience of stones.
Ah! I miss that small window above the door
where I used to hide cats eyes, I mean marbles.

I miss so much the view to trees from there.
I want to go up again on a barrel to that window
and drop in on the faithful traces of my hands.
Yes, my hands which groped
for everything precious I hid in there.
My hands hugging each other now as I sit
in the dark burning on my own with nostalgia.
No one burns with me except my cigarette.
Oh ink, no one would save me but you
Oh ink, take me to the vivid images of life,
keep me away, far away from "the dead."

New Life

By Emmanuel Ikuoye

Heavenly bodies rejoice
Flowers open, seas overflow banks
Joyous roses flood the streets
Mortal being in love again

Nightingales sing, thunder claps
Mother Earth beaming with smiles
Her child now feels warmth of touch
Happy rain falls, sorrow gone

Tears of joy rush like freed floods
Burdens lifted, heart lightened
Cage broken, captive set free
Laughter echoes in the vale

Lions, tigers kowtow, dazzled
For two hearts melted in one
True love found, sparkling life sprung
Running streams serenade night

Hand in Hand

By Ashley O'Keefe

Harps play from the heavens
Angels strum their strings,
Waves scroll up the shore
The angels spread their wings...

... Across the mists of dawn
Within its gossamer veil,
Two lovers meet, they kiss, they greet
Run off along the trail,

Two hearts hold their stories
Both run hand in hand,
Down to the beach, in search, they breach
Make sweet love upon the sand,

Harps play from the heavens
Angels strum their strings,
Waves scroll up the shore
In the salty air, love sings...

... Two lost and lonely people
Wash up on the shore,
Hand in hand upon the sand
Together forevermore,

Harps play from the heavens
Angels strum their strings...

I Had a Great Time

By Brian Keith

I'll see you in silence
When out goes the light
I'll pour out my sympathy
When you give up the fight

I'll stand with your body
To say my goodbyes
But I simply cannot see
Your soul in your eyes

You lay there still
I feel your grace
My mind can't understand
The empty look on your face

Please don't be fearful
I just seen the end
For the man that lay sill
Is your very close friend

So now that it's over.
I can see all my sins
The body I spoke of
Is me to my friends

I rise up to the heavens
To leave you all behind
But please don't you worry
I had a great time.

The Last House on Delaney

By Karen Bessette

I always loved the dead end streets,
especially the last house on Delaney.
Here the wildflowers danced in
the untamed grass and the birds sang
on the old worn out picket fence.
I stayed here for quite a while
listening to the birds sing and
comforted by the bright sun above me.

Are You, Can You, When We, I Know

By Brian Keith

Are you working on your anger
Are you quiet in the weeds
Are you alone in your sorrow
Are you the one planting seeds

Can you run from danger
Can you see the horror still
Can you feel the growing tension
Can you see or shoot to kill

When we know the end is near
When we lay silent on the ground
When we drop bombs that kill by millions
When we hope some life can still be found

I know the bleak is old and tripe
I know the end when foretold before
I know you hear the media it tells you
I know it's all worse than just before

(Are you) all surprised by this
(Can you) tell pandemics are not so new
(When) war has been waged so many times
(I know) this all because it's coming true

Mindless Sea

By Vincent Blaison

Drifting away in a mindless sea
Clarity is sometimes clouded
As my mind gets a hold of me
Searching for what?
As if it is not already held within
The sculptor's block
Chiselling

Drowned rocks
Once a part of me
As their ripples slowly fade
The water stills...
I am found within the block
Direction of shade
Persuaded by light
Change the focus
To see the purpose
The mist begins to clear
Direction
Once again in sight

Oracles

By Tom Cleary

A sterile sodden sun salutes a grim greedy globe
at the broken dawn.
Flights of falcons, fertile fields flowing in the wind
found at one time a fortune
are no more.
Glistening of green
once nature's own denomination
has been devalued to a few denuded leafy denizens
as impoverished forested favelas fumbling for relief
find but drips of donated dollars
just to dig roots into banks of ravished rotted rivers
an aborted afterthought in avarice.
Crows, for centuries the sentries of oracular occurrences
always able to read faces and future phases
foretell man's famine
for without our mother
we are fish without fins
birds in broken wings
naked shivering winter trees
never to bloom
yet we persist in our belief
we are our own gods.

Soulful Sunflowers

By Melanie Garfinkle Waknine

In a field of sunflowers
cheerful and gay
almost hypnotic
they were gazing my way.
Perfect petals
attracting the heat—
large green leaves
contending to compete.
Standing up straight
Nature's modelling show—
a side to side dance
as the wind started to blow.
Like a million happy faces
on a star studded screen,
these natural beauties
a floral lover's dream.
Season ends
stalks are aching...
Though,
there is no mistaking;
the two tone fields
green and yellow—
will lie bare barren
and fallow.
Once again
when summer arrives
they will reinvent
their 'happy go lucky' lives...
Oh! Glorious flowers
now I stare at you—
when you smile at me
I will revive and renew.

another place and time

By John Thornton

can't help myself
i sit and watch
who could you be
my wandering thought
a stranger you are
have we met before
in another place
i need to know more
are we two wings
of the same bird
maybe so true
almost drifts unheard
but still i stare
can you hear
it's a previous life
drawing us near
i remember you now
was a simpler time
but not just once
our many lives entwine

Morning Greeting

By Ryan Bates

Here upon the wooden pathway
Moss adorns the trail so thickly
Emerald greens through ancient forests
Every step is moist and sticky
Slowly walking 'round the corners
No direction is displaying
Listen to the breezes flowing
Through the leaves as trees are swaying
Sunlight beams between their branches
Gently while the birds are singing
Flying all around the foliage
Such a lovely morning greeting

Life's Debris

By Kenneth Drysdale

I'm cluttered in life's debris
Does it reveal my seductive eyes?
I need to be in the front seat
Do my doubts fuel my faithful cries?
Does it reveal my seductive eyes?
Sparkling trinkets of self-defeat
Do my doubts fuel my faithful cries?
Wall of trust form a gate to retreat
Sparkling trinkets of self-defeat
I need to be in the front seat
Wall of trust form a gate to retreat
I'm cluttered in life's debris

catch myself

By John Thornton

i catch myself
oldness grows
lines on a face
how it shows
i catch myself
stood in the rain
what's it about
it's love it's pain
i catch myself
a younger one
was a different day
that's long gone
i catch myself
was just a dream
no understanding
what does it mean
i catch myself
somewhere else
obliviously uncertain
like time itself

We Lost the World

By Steve Wheeler

So softly out those words can trip
  as we run from the flicking whip
Feed from the trough, take one more sip
  and hear the planet's fabric rip
The fat cats grasping, paranoid
  while we, as men like mice avoid
the darkest, coldest outer void
  and blame it all on Sigmund Freud

Oh what a tangled web we weave
  Oh how we weep, oh how we grieve
What meagre earnings we receive
  yet still, in profits we believe
What knives! What bloody handed tools
  we brandish as the furnace cools!
But we are nothing more than fools
  to trample over precious jewels

We rape the ruins of our lands
  and drain the life from foreign strands
We shrug as our malaise expands
  and wash the guilt from off our hands
We turn to dross, to worthless drips
  of tainted pleasure, touching lips
But all runs through our fingertips
  before the ultimate eclipse
I cannot look, I must despair
  to watch us choke in poisoned air
We turned our backs on something rare
  and chose the darkness of the lair

So blind, it makes me want to screech!
  It take away my power of speech
We had salvation in our reach
  but nothing could our spirits teach
Nothing could convince our minds
  that truth, in red, was underlined

and waiting there for us to find
  but we were happy to stay blind

Now Earth groans louder in its pain
  as slowly rotting hills of grain
foreground the quickly growing stain
  of toxic clouds and acid rain
and deep inside our febrile brains
  we hum the same old, tired refrain
that's slowly driving us insane:

We lost the world; what did we gain?

Red Rose

By Sarfraz Ahmed

The veins of the rose
Expose the love
So deep that it shadows
My world as I walk
In darkness without you.
Blood red palpitating and pure
Love that was once unsure
Is now beating
Defiant in this heart of mine
Blistered in thorns
Blood red
It shines
Beautiful in a love divine.
Fragranced and tender
In fragments
Deep-rooted sophistication
Penetrated colours
In the love I feel for you
Leaving me breathless
Fading in the wind
Blooded in tormenting cries
As another red rose blooms and dies.

The Lost Jeté

By Yanny Widjanarko

Expressions float in the timeline that has no metre
Crawling on the walls of various shapes of wounds
Where phrases stalled until the gate of oral
Where missing and remorse dwell within her manipulative attic.
This is the hall where she made the show
The place to perform her fiction dance, solo
Where she is the entertainer and the audience
Where paradigm and feelings collide, made the other senses
She plucked the faults that destined not to be forgotten
Enshrined by every second of remaining molecular
Feelings were shredded, exhibition exfoliated
Yet, she's a flesh that stays whole for a quaint diorama
The enigmas burgeoning, slipped through her fingers
Creating every stroke of her canvas
Her transitory abstractions
Melts from her mind to her lips
Yet, smothered by the shades of disbelieve
Her pattern is clear
She climbed through dust and was lost in the wind.

In the Thawing Heat

By Stewart Musiwa

In the thawing heat
Of an African winter midday
Hopelessly he lies, blood cold
Where on a deaf rich man's gateway
He had spent the chilly night
Scavenge for crumbs he might
Like the Biblical poor man
The rich master's dogs he befriends
And they bring him morsels they can
And in sympathy lick his wounds;
On judgement day the poor man will not fear
But the rich man will cry for Lazarus to hear.

When I Was Alone

By Marten Hoyle

I asked myself a question,
When I was alone,
The answer was unknown.
I see the people as they come
To the hollow funeral drum.
They come in masks of horror
With voices of distant thunder.
Tell me—are they happy?
Do they know I am sorry?
Can I trust this as a memory?
Are these things that only I see?
Is yesterday what it seems,
Or am I just remembering my dreams?
Lone lives longing to be lost—
Pretty flowers dying in the frost.
When will you ever come home?

Soon, you'll be a memory,
Sleeping sound in storm clouds
Of another yesterday.
Soon, we'll say our goodbyes—goodbyes
Because everybody dies.

You'll be just moonbeams, and tears.
Why must you fade like the rainbows
In tired mists over the trees?
I must have lost you
Like a bird on the horizon,

Soaring through the twilight
That hurts my tired eyes.
You were weeping through my soul
When I said I cannot walk beside you
Through the fields of your visions
To the far side of slumber
Where we'd recall what we were dreaming.

They came in masks of horror
To bear you through the heartache—

Past the sepulcher where our forms lie
Beyond the iron gates of sorrow
To leave me to my endless sleep,
Aching in my dreams of your voice,
So like the waves of a dying sea.

And all the night long, I lie in pain
Feeling I will know you, never again.
Such is sleep...such is sleep...

Warm Istanbul Nights

By Sarfraz Ahmed

Beautified in the moment
Your gestures drew me in
Flesh to flesh
Skin to skin
You ignited a flame
When you touched my hand
When you held me close
When we held each other's hands
As we danced on dust and sand
Our bodies moved
Hearts intertwined
Smiles and laughter
Spread like fine wine
As you lifted me higher
Each touch electrified
Spread like wildfire.
Captivated me
Breathed life into me
Two people
That found a way to connect
On those warm Istanbul Nights.

Where the Peaceful Waters Flow

By Patti Woosley

He came to me one starlit night
and he took hold of my hand.
We soared to places far away
to a faraway, distant land.

Flying high among the whitest clouds,
beyond the skies so blue.
Such wonders I had never seen before.
Such splendors I never knew.

Into a storm so fierce and wild;
more than my heart could stand.
He said, "Don't fear, my precious child,
just keep holding onto my hand."

A silver moon was shining bright.
A trillion stars lit up our way.
High into the starry sky,
we soared to a brand new day.

Miles before we reached the gates,
sweet music filled the skies.
A chorus of ten thousand angels
was singing praises to the Lord on high.

The gates unlocked and opened up,
and with an angel as my guide,
the Light all at once filled my heart.
Such joy I felt inside.

The clearest waters I had ever seen,
flowed in streams beyond compare.
Beautiful flowers grew in grassy fields.
Trees and birds were everywhere.

I saw everyone who I had ever loved.
I was overwhelmed with joyful tears,
and I found the peace I'd been searching for,
as His love replaced my fears.

And I didn't want to ever leave
and go back to the world below,
for my heart yearned to stay with God
where the peaceful waters flow.

essence of being a kid

By Audrine Max

we always talk about
the good old days
back in our younger years
before adulthood and maturity
come to think of it
when we were young
we weren't deluded too much
of false beliefs
the negative was not as strong
we always had a happy
youthful perspective
as our grandparents say
back in our days
when the world was better
here we are now
saying the same lines
telling others
times have changed
but- time is merely
a witness
on the arrangement
of our minds
taking a different perspective
we call it now an adult's
not that of an innocent child
how far along
did we mentally travel
from seeing mostly good
to coping with

life's everyday disputes
so i strive to be
a kid at heart, meek
peering into life
through rose tinted spectacles
for lucky are the meek
as they will inherit heaven
for the meek are strong
not what is now believed
it is rather marked
with unwavering belief,
faith, joy, hope, and expectancy
child, be brave enough
to carry much
of those qualities
perhaps you'll see a world
more beautiful, colorful
like it was or better
than before
so train yourself
to recapture the essence
of being a kid.

Keeper

By Tom Cleary

An inveterate angler
viewing my tackle box of brightly tied flies
poetic phrases, images, fragments
ready to be sunk into the depths of cranial rivers
away from conscious daylight
where surface shadows can spook
sharpened to snag a glistening gem
shining radiantly through the third eye
reeling out, I expend our energies
playing our strengths to exhaustion
until it flops warm and tender
rainbow trout of inner truth
sizzling on heated page.

My Child is Dead

By Brandon Adam Haven

My child is dead
before I could ever meet
My child is dead
never did I get to see

My child has gone
So far away from me
My child has gone
But still my heart does bleed

Does my angel yet live
In clouds above and high
Does my angel yet live
Or in blackness do they reside

Is my child alive
Looking down on me as I cry
Is my child alive
As I struggle through this life

Is my child next to me
In some soulful form
Is my child next to me
To let me know I'm not alone

Is my child with The Lord
Joyful and chuckling away?
Is my child with The Lord
Awaiting patiently for me?

Shall I welcome my last breath
Each day I still feel the dread?
Shall I welcome my last breath?
For my sweet child is dead

Desire

By André Field

So, you want desire:
each pore tingling
with electric fire.
No problem!
I can do desire.
Look at my eyes
and you'll see it there,
hungry and burning,
undisguised.
So what, if I know
it's what you need?
There's no contract
guaranteed.
It's not a secret
plan or ruse—
not a tactic
that I use.
It's that I see
it's what you need
that draws out this
desire in me.
The mirror of
your own desire
that lights the deep
primeval fire.
And this passion
joins us both,
knowing what
we both need most.
Two passions cut
from a single cloth—
we are each other's candle;
we are each other's moth.

Thoughts on Ukraine

By André Field

(i) Stalker

Although we divorced more than 30 years ago,
Now I realise that you'll never let me go.
In those early years, you know, it wasn't all that bad,
The settlement was working: we were living side by side.
You even guaranteed that you would help look after me,
In return for when I left your nuclear family.
Some years ago, a change occurred, a stranger on the scene:
A suitor with his promise of a European dream.
He offered untold riches, and I found my head was turned,
Which left you feeling belittled, inadequate, and spurned.
So, you became my stalker and you gave me no more rest,
Because I built my new house with its windows facing west.
There is no court of law and there's no restraining decree,
And there's no power that can stop you from molesting me.
You marched right in and took my home and said that I was
yours,
And that you wanted to go back to how things were before.
But I will fight you every night to show that we are through:
That it is your possessiveness that makes me detest you.

(ii) Plague

It's like a plague
Of biblical proportions.
But it's no Godly rage,
Or divine extortion.
Daubs of blood on lintels and walls
Are daubs of pain, injustice and war.

Locusts of hate,
And locusts of vanity:
A swarm at the gate
Of peace and humanity.
Total destruction of all in its path
Swathes of sorrow when at last it has passed.

What kind of mind
Of febrile insanity,
Like an angry spoiled child
Whose lust knows no boundary?
Just a little grey man with cold bulging eyes,
And delusions of grandeur and a sackful of lies.

She Danced with a Stranger

By Lisa Combs Otto

She danced with a stranger,
their hearts became friends.
Fires raged.
Vulnerability burned to the ground.
Souls merged.
Falling became part of their dance.
And she will never dance
with another stranger again.

Jerusalem

By André Field

And where are England's pastures green?
Bleached bare in the Saharan drought.
And what became of English dreams?
Will all her promise come to nowt?
Can you conceive a lamb so pure
Would ever tread upon these hills,
Whose clouds leave lost ideals obscure,
Are these the dark satanic mills?
And where now is that golden bow,
And where my arrows of desire,
What can I do; where can I go
Without a chariot of fire?
Now England turns to dust and sand,
And all my hopes are torn apart,
There is no green and pleasant land,
Or Jerusalem in my heart.

Hidden Serenity

By Kenneth Drysdale

Verdant sea crept, nourishing
Photosynthesis stirring
Alien planet, genetic stream
Secluded life, Everest dream
Clouds caress soulful wings
Glorified praise, cherubim sings
Absorbing prayers, faceted seams
Moments cherished, smearing themes
Born protection, shiny bark
Stories told, rainbow spark
Fika existence, enlightened regime
Blinking seraphim supreme
Peaceful ring, desires wean
Microscopic teeth obscene
Trudging past aeons of screams
Internal love redeems

The Fields Gaze

By Steve Wheeler

As the hours give life, the fields gaze oh so gently
We glow in hallowed flesh, but only for a while
Sometimes we sing, our melodies ring silently
I trade my torments for your simple smile

Rainbowed deck chairs, where the sun seeks lethargy
Flowers and fields in temperate breezes fly
Transparently aware, they rise so nonchalantly
While juicy peaches swell so slowly in July

Why did the summer melt; to find its distance?
For each day triumphs in rejuvenated hours
There's beauty found with the sun's expanses
Then hurriedly we shelter from the summer showers

Candescent Moon

By Charlene Phare

Dark tangerine skies, sultry hue
Developing deeper with time
Twilight hours fading out of sight
Wax melting to our hearts delight
Seductive healing, tastes divine

Earth receiving her blessings
Offers repetitive refrain
Shedding grace to every creature
Solace, peace, her redeeming feature
Tender touching kisses, purest rain

Eventide, solitude thoughts bestowed
Glorious elements emulated
Translucent clouds strongly embellished
Ever changing seasons, replenished
Love for mother nature, she's cherished
Temperature levels, regulated

Panoramic views, atmospheric
Electric ambience created
Rolling tides interrupted silence
Stunning beauty complete decadence
Denying any contrivance
Leaving onlookers breath abated

Shadows formed over the horizon
Tricoloured picture brightly shining
Gradual transformations underway
Sunsetting from just another day
World slumbering, having to convey
Harmoniously combining

Striving to realise own dreams
Borrowed souls, lives over too soon
All footprints deeply imprinted
Collective stories depicted
Our legacies live on conscripted
As we gaze at the candescent moon

Can't You See Her?

Emmanuel Ikuoye

There is poetry everywhere
She is in my brain, heartbeats
In my chamber, the garden, roses
Dancing dandelions
Can't you see her?

Poetry everywhere
The chirping crickets
Thrushes blasting the vale, butterflies hovering
Snakes hissing

Rainbows smiling
Clouds receding
Thunder clapping
Lightning flashing
Storms raging, cool breeze refreshing
She is beasts wild and mild
Humans lettered or not, boisterous or moody,
Tall and short

Poetry in wartimes
Manifests during peace
The splashing, blue oceans
The gentle flowing river
The beautiful meadows, evergreen scenery
In cities elegant and sophisticated,
hamlets simple and stunning
Climes crude and refined

There is poetry in dark, silent nights
Starry skies, scalding days, freezing moments,
in life's ravines, mountains
Life is poetry
All forms of poetry
Greatest tutors for all seasons
Delights to souls
Can't you see her?

The Dark Planet

By Aaron Blackie

Oh, Dark Planet,
Sits cross-legged
On the seat of your throne
Far in the region of

Vagueness,
Island of darkness
Un-scanned,
Of cloudiness untamed
In obtuse angle
To the planetary
System, revolving
Round rolls
Of the mysterious
And the mystical...

Darkened planet!
Abode of deep blackness,
Dangling troubles
That came surging
Like swamping locusts
Flying on feathers
With pronounced fingers –
Of the wasters
Of the emptier
In the wild with
Clandestine boots...

Are you not weary
Of pouring out on all,
Those wastes to
No end,
Those empties to
No rend?

Blurry images in shadows
Painting the

Human landscapes,
Cacophonic voices
Of miseries and anguishes...

Across your wrinkled face
Shadowy forms of
Creeping creatures,
Camouflages of miseries
Trailing earth-bound;
All submerged in the
Dominion of darkness...

But out of the trailing
Clouds of darkness,
The wonders of light
Are birthed
On the plightful laps
Of earth upheavals...

For the wary
Humanity
Is light-entuned
Darkness-repulsed
Hope-attuned...
Out of thick darkness,
The colour
Of light is brightened

And the mortally
wounded pathways
Are lighted
On to the dawn of
A new day,
Of a new season:
The good always
Over the evil...

Don't Hide, Little Wallflower

By George Valler

Don't hide among the bushes
One day all the leaves will fall
Just climb up through the branches
To make yourself feel tall
For life can be a blessing
As well as a blesséd curse
By climbing tall, before a fall
Your way above the worst
Just embrace the joy of living
This miracle that is you
Just remember who you are
You're a million among the few
Don't hide among the bushes
One day the leaves will fall

Raven Night

By Joan Audette

Raven night swallows me
in its cavernous embrace.
Endless echoes question,
only to be met with stagnant replies.
Staggering stillness...
no lilting music of life.
Where has all my sunshine gone?
Shadows momentarily free the moon.
I see the willow;
it weeps for me.

Solace-on-Sea

By Graeme Stokes

The affable ripples of the coming tide,
roll in on a summer's breeze
In my seat I'm reclined, I note the dwindling sand,
kiss the glistening sea
From my privileged vantage, I capture nature at work,
gifting colour to my vapid canvas
Seagulls screech with unrestrained delight,
liberated in their elevated status
Dog and master lap up the rampant freedom,
giddy on a tranquil high
Dog shakes lose watery excess, barks out a zest for life
The whoosh of distant traffic, the metronomic hum,
kept safely at arm's length
A world away from my peaceful space,
my sea, my sky, my bench!
The ever fickle shape-shifting clouds, profits
on the expectant horizon
Tell of fresh wheels turning for dormant ambitions,
openings to cast an eye on
From scrunched up face, I spy the plane above,
dishing out a merited break
I clamp down on the contrails, and savour the cathartic state
As the hours evaporate in the sands of time, I exhale and
slowly rise
Until we meet again therapeutic, I'll bring me, myself and I!

Across the Sea

By Stevan Lyman

Somewhere out there, way across the sea,
She sits on the shore, just waiting for me..
Looking up at the stars, longing for true love,
As a silhouette appears, in the dark sky above..
She looks down at the picture she holds in her hand,

Has a loving warm feeling, as she starts to understand..
One day he will be here,
so we can hold each other tight,
But just for now, it's another lonely night..
Her dreams forever closer, as each day passes by,
And then a teardrop appears,
in the corner of her eye..
Then she looks up again, and the silhouette has gone,
She whispers "Goodnight my love,
we will be together someday"
"I promise you my true love, it won't be long..."

The Pillars of the Earth

By George Valler

I came into this world
With really nothing at all
Except a Mother's love
wrapped in a baby's shawl

She was to be my forward life
And me to be her all
I was this little tiny mite
That could answer to her call

My mother was my guiding light
She taught me right from wrong
And for whatever else
She taught me to be strong

Life cut for me a different slice
From a different cake each day
And stepping stones laid out the path
To send me on my way

Tears in her eyes I did not see
As I strode off into life

To find, she knew, another hand
She knew to be a wife

I walked the forward stony path
Doors opened and doors closed
And what lay hidden, corners deep
No one, well, really knows

Sometimes the streets seem golden
Sometimes as black as Hell
How often had one too take it
No matter how life fell

Strength was to be my saviour
Wrapped in life's loving shawl
And memories of a Mother strong
A Mother who gave it all

Dreamscaping

By Sarah Tillbrook

To the world beyond a dream
Beyond a stream
Beyond a book

That journeys further than the clouds
Have ever seen
Too far to look

And see, the formally unseen
It's not a dream
It's daylight fantasy

As we're left on a hook
And off to sleep
To words antiquity.

One Glorious Autumn Day

By Patti Woosley

We went to the park with the boys
one Glorious Autumn Day.
The skies were blue, the sun was shining,
and the wonders of Nature were on display.

A mama duck was swimming;
her ducklings behind her in formation.
Flocks of geese were flying overhead
to some tropical destination.

We ate our lunch beneath the trees,
while gathering leaves up off the ground.
Some had turned from green to red,
and some from gold to brown.

Little sparrows were eating leftover bread;
their tiny heads bobbing up and down.
I sat on a bench and watched the boys
chasing their Grandpa all around.

From across the park, I saw a young man,
coming around from the other side.
He had a familiar stride that made me decide,
I hoped he would stop by.

As he got closer, my heart stood still
as he sweetly kissed my hand.
"It's me, Mom," he said, with a gentle smile.
"I came today to help you understand."

"I know you're sad, but I want you to know,
I am always very near.
Please take care of my boys until they are grown.
Then, you can come and meet me here."

I opened my eyes from the sweetest dream.

I smiled because I felt such peace.
My son had visited me in my sleep
and in that moment, my sadness ceased.

I walked around and found the boys
throwing rocks into a pond.
Their Grandpa and I felt so very blessed
holding their hands as we walked home.

Later that night, my little grandson whispered in my ear.
"I saw him too," he said.
"He blew a kiss and waved to me.
I saw you with my Dad."

Day's End

By Christian Ryan Pike

Underneath the wash
Of golden evening atmosphere
Soaking in the shades of light
Sprinkled with the stars of night
Like a dreamy liquid in the sheen
Of gradients of glowing
Precious lavender with auburn in between
In my captivation I can gaze
Free of all the cumbersome
Necessity that weighs
Pulling at my weakness all my days
But still enlightened by
The rapturing composure of a luminescent sky
Alleviated, such that I could cry
To see from such a tiny bit of soil
The handiwork of heaven
And of my Creator's toil
I tremble as the angels dry the ink
Afraid to miss the angles
And so careful not to blink
In knowing that what seems to be, to me

The overwhelming pressure
Is dissolved in glassy sea
Of radiant celestial delight
I reach my heart and hand
Though I could never reach the height
And nothing else can matter in its sight
I'm satisfied to matter
And exist in my own right

wear it proudly

By Audrine Max

relief is what I feel
every time I dwell not
in logic and reasoning
but in the comforts
and safety
of my imagination
where the visions
had been fulfilled
as He has prepared
the mansion, the state
that carries all possibilities
in which the aim
has been attained
for the conceiver
and the conception
are one and the same

there is only freedom
from the bondage
of the surface mind
every time I
feel the soul
of every word
I have seeded
in the depths
of my subconscious
happiness is

what i gain
love flows freely
every day is wonderful
there is no need
to escape
no reason to leave
only a gentle reminder
to which state I am
mentally dwelling
as i love wearing
that sort of fragrance
throughout the day
letting the idea permeate
so every cell in my body
is consumed
possessed by it

oh sweet success
whilst sitting
at the mountain of serenity
I can live like this
every day
fidelity and loyalty
to my Being's aim
the only thing
it is asking of me
is to trust
have faith
live boldly, joyfully
let the seed germinate
let it sprout
its first branches and leaves

patience dear
keep projecting
and soon you'll see
all the beauty
you have
created within
so wear those jewels proudly.

Hey Soldier!

By Graeme Stokes

I stand before you soldier!
Clothes hanging from shattered bones
My family now resides in Jannah
On Earth?... A shell I once called home!
Do my cold eyes freeze you?
A resolve… that belies my tender years
The wail of the sirens scream daily
The roar of bombs mark the killing fields
Do you think you can break me soldier?
When I have little left to lose
The madness has ceased to faze me
Now I walk in bitter shoes!
I see you shifting furtively
Biting hard on nervous lips
I'm scavenging for scraps of your desert soul
For an oasis where empathy sips!
I don't hate you soldier!
Although I surely should
Horrors a child should never see
A family prostrate in wood
Did I detect you wavering?
A flicker in that clinical face
I refuse to falter, withdraw my stare
Unless you respect my place!
I will pray for you smart soldier
Assault rifle and bayonet
With the call to prayer comes sunrise
From decimated minarets
I pray your own, sleep sound tonight
They do when they're loved you see?
I long for a hug, a bedtime story
A mother to hold tight to me!
As Salaam Alaikum soldier
Even though you've seen me wrong!
Will there come a day when you reciprocate
With Wa Alaikum Salaam?

Den of Dreams

By Ryan Bates

Follow me to the den of dreams,
Come listen to the sparrows sing
Their songs of hope so cheerfully
As they rest along the trail

Merciful is the morning sun
Go gather to her precious ones
Through rays of love for everyone
As she rises on the dell

Beautiful are the flowers bloom
Sweet fragrance from the gardens loom
Around the grounds like soft perfume
To relax your weary soul

Oncoming is a gentle breeze
So rhythmic have become the leaves
They rattle high within the trees
Here upon the wooded knoll

Motionless is the healing lake
Look fondly to it's warm embrace
As sunshine does illuminate
the reflections crystal clear

Echoes of crackling come from the woods
Slow rustling trampled under hoof
With bonds complete in brotherhood
Comes a herd of whitetail deer

Poem for Fallen Wives

By Andrew Kerr Shaw

You have gone into a room
Where black furniture lines the walls
that are draped in thick raven curtains
And where the carpet is as dark as the deepest pond.
Above the room a black light sprinkles darkness
Further into its square of midnight
Cutting off the room, beside it, where I stand and wait.
I have studied the lock and know
that many before me have tried to turn
That pitch black keyhole
Which changes its shape with every turn.
I am Orpheus and you are Eurydice
But where he failed,
I have made a skeleton key that is
as white as bone with our lives
Etched into its shape and form –
That will bewilder Death and change its shape
To open the lock.
I shall tear away all that is black in the room
where you are camouflaged
And hidden in ink
So that when the black tidal wave tries to pull you back
I have another key to another room
Where foxgloves and wildflowers grow
Where we can be safe and live again.

Pools of Tranquillity

By Ryan Bates

Pristine cascades
Untouched by many
Trickling down
Into pools of plenty

From every surface
Drips sweet symphony
Collecting cool currents
of tranquillity

Among the stones
Hidden by trees
Radiant sun comes
Shining through leaves

On the smooth stones
Where thick moss grows
Luscious and green
And soft to the toes

Sitting beside
The waters streaming
Watching warm
Golden sunset gleaming

Stasis (in Monochrome)

By Jimmy Ray Davis

Silhouettes of steam
whisper languidly.
Maddening how life
trudges on,
mindless of this misery
etched into my soul.
You see, my world is frozen
all I have chosen,
shadows of faded memories.
Since your love
said goodbye
to me.

Street lamps glow with warmth.
Children run and play
unaware of the pain
that will replace yesterday.
Shops are open for business
bustlers trundle through
every door.
I remain in stasis
refugee of the unseen.
Since your love
said goodbye
to me.

I walk as if in a dream.
Surreal how everything slows
and my feet hesitate
without a destination,
nowhere left to go.
Like many who've traversed
a cursed path
I mumble hello and nod
Passers-by oblivious
to eyes
that cried
all of the night before.

Car horns blaring, daring
to shatter a birdsong.
So many vibrant colors
alive, smothering my senses.
I walk in monochrome
a drone amid the kaleidoscape.
Cannot escape the feeling
fate is stealing my essence.
Hence, I meander lost
since your love
said goodbye
to me.

Cinnamon Dreams

By Charlene Phare

Cinnamon dreams, savoury with sweet
Warm delicate tones permeating
Smoother than chocolate, delicious treat

Captured flavours, admitting defeat
Delicacies penetrating
Cinnamon dreams, savoury with sweet

Fanning down flames from constant heat
Spices mixing, amalgamating
Smoother than chocolate, delicious treat

Drifting aromas subtly repeat
Sugared rush, sudden palpitating
Cinnamon dreams, savoury with sweet

Burning desires, will never retreat
Divine taste devoured, salivating
Smoother than chocolate, delicious treat

Enhanced condiments, meal complete
Their hungry eyes exaggerating
Smoother than chocolate, delicious treat
Cinnamon dreams, savoury with sweet

Bond

By R. David Fletcher

In the dusk of a dying day she sits,
Eyes glistening in the rays,
She peers at a photo of our lives,
Immersed in childhood days.

Her fingers caress the embroidered frame,
Touching the visage there,
My private bond is now complete,
A father's hope and prayer.

The Faces of the Wind

By Kristina Bray

The wind speaks quietly tonight upon the cliff tops bare.
It sighs like a contented child who slumbers without care.
To hear it caressing the waves you would not ever think
It is the same foul, wild tempest that causes ships to sink
And makes the sailors' lovers rise to pray their menfolk home
Beseeching God not to let them be smothered by the foam.
You would not imagine it roars about the lighthouse round
And makes the night-time creatures shrink in terror at the sound
Or that it beats the tree branches until they're forced to fall
Or the trunks, with a heartfelt groan, sink downward, roots and all.
No evil of the current gentle hush would you believe
For it seems to want only serenity to achieve.
Yet both the tempests are as one, the terror and the grace.
Both of them lie within its range, both live in the same place.
Two such opposing camps yet lie in men as well as air.
The extremes need not damage aught, as long as we're aware
That, though we may bluster, we need to seek the place between
The fury and the silence, the space where we are serene.
We're made to dwell in that bright space where
the sunshine glows high
To watch the birds soar on the wind and circle through the sky.
Only rarely should we allow ourselves to howl and blow
And seldom let ourselves relax in ease upon life's flow.
Doing so, we have the best chance of a life filled with joy.
By walking on the centre path we've power to enjoy
More than if we choose to be devoured or to devour.
Be like a summer wind, blow gently on each little flower.

The Wolves of Nav

By Rosario Aurelius

As I explained the history of the crest,
and the symbols we all once wore,
He divided the air between us,
with the silvered edge of his sword,

"Our lineage was working class,
something you will never understand,"
Thank you, I said, for mansplaining
this shifting sand beneath our feet,
that dissolves the vines and roots from before,
"No Luv," I declared, "Our people were victims of war!"
They chose sides,
not for the payment tyrants provide,
but for the power and security
that lifted us from impurity,
We were not all Tito,
bearing baskets of severed heads to the nationalist regime,
We were not all kissed
by the inspiration of Dracul's phalanx gardens unclean,
Our mothers and fathers were wolves
who fled the fields where no corpse may hide,
The roots of the forests stained in the auld crimson tide,
Who travelled by the sea aside
for a garden of promise and peace swept by,
who became soldiers of a different regime,
mercenaries who fertilized the garden
with the blood of other men's dreams.

Never was our ancestry defined
by the tyrants who paid our wages with blood money,
Miners, messengers, mercenaries, manpower,
slaves building the pyramids for a modern monarchy,
Men-made sold lies about familial honor.

Our wolves lay hidden in caverns of filthy dales,
tufts of fur torn, wounded with scarlet veils,
whose ears perked up, listen to the howling winds sway
their bellies close to the earth, terror held at bay,
Panting, breathing in soft rewards,
just before they were loosed, as dogs of war,
The hands of no-man may soothe these ravenous jaws,
or silence the mawing of the howling beast,
Gathered from the verdant orchards
and golden fields of summer's everlong idyllic feast.

Where Are You?

By Jimmy Ray Davis

They're lined up around the block
to fly on your Ferris Wheel.
Can't say I blame them much,
for I know what they feel.
Broken angels watch on
with their crumpled wings.
They say there's a place in hell,
where a church bell rings.
But I walked away.
from the jail of your charm.
For it's only when you bite the apple
that you find the worm.
Do they lie, do they seethe?
shaking heads in unison..
Yet I know the way.
Yes I know where the path begins.

So just close your eyes.
Don't take it the wrong way.
Sometimes mortal goodbyes,
are just whispers from the grave.
Bladeless axe handles
still hurt in the wrong hands.
Did you really think
this was all you could stand.
Will you scream? Will you bleed?
Will you find what you need?
In this cruel world
where life is for dreamers.

I've paved your broken road
but I can't bear the load.
Lies and love are the same
in your heart's fragile abode.
Where are you?
Where are you right now?
Where are you?

Hiding in your red house.
Do you know? Do you think?
Pour yourself another drink.
Come out to play
I'll find the way.
What will you do?
Just give me a clue.
Honey where
are
...You?

The Legendary Wordsmith

By Peter William Levi

You'll hear this wondrous myth,
The rapidly rhyming Wordsmith,
Slyly saying such syllables with,
His brutally blunt accurate pith.
Voicing a vocabulary very vast,
He's fluent in flowing facts fast,
Spinning some smooth sayings,
Slick sentence showing slayings.
An unreadable word combination,
Cloaks such sensitive Information,
Has a mastery in communication,
And using this hypnotic sensation,
Helps people find their destination.
Many marvellously claimed to be the
Legendary wordsmith, But I think the
Mastermind is merely a myth. I'll do a
Monumental masterpiece, I don't need
No turdsmith, I'm a powerful poet player
Ponder pith. So searching through sweet
Sentences and finding the silky smooth
Saying, so some Sayer starts shouting,
Wordsmith! Wordsmith! Wordsmith!

Natural Fractals

By Charlene Phare

Souls' inner patterns revealing
Pulses, waves, connectivity
Pandora's box concealing

Solitude complexity
Pulses, waves, connectivity
Blood rushes urgently through our veins
Solitude complexity
Yet our natural fractals remain
Blood rushes urgently through our veins
Adrenaline a steady pump
Yet our natural fractals remain
Riding waves, the occasional bump
Adrenaline a steady pump
Intricately designed machines
Recovering from every bump
Continuing with our own routines
Intricately designed machines
Destiny struck its final blow
Continuing with own routines
Internal love nurtured, grow
Destiny struck its final blow
Visions could not be retracted
Internal love had to grow
Black merged with white, contrasted
Visions never to be retracted
Dispersed den of iniquity
Black merged with white, contrasted
Replenished stores of serenity

Silent Screams

By Graeme Stokes

I stare!
They look away
Heads down
Eyes reluctant to Play
Society in decay!
The rumbling of the train, plays a requiem for broken dreams
Hollow shells grasp for life drifting on a dark foreboding stream
Through the encompassing malaise, souls emit a silent scream!
Books and phones, a fortification against the stark reality
Brakes screech a vehement protest, a voice in the stifling banality
"Trespassers Will Be Prosecuted!" Arms folded tight, a wall of brooding hostility
Crushed spirits in an arid wilderness, cry a plea for long lost passions
Brusque nods and furtive glances, the afforded meagre rations
Faces lined with tension, tell tales of gruelling regimes
Puppets in the system, cogs in the wheel of the corporate machine
Collective shuffles of unease, sit aside incoherent ramblings
A scapegoat for the masses, a deflection from their own circumstances
Errant bags effect anxious scrutiny from timorous minds in a fractured community
Subconsciously lamenting for a bygone unity
The optimistic declaration proclaims colourfully titled stations
Delusive images manifest of rich and vibrant destinations
I probe for life from torpid minds
I search for smiles from lethargic eyes
Silent screams masquerade as apathetic yawns
Death by a Thousand Cuts from recurrent dawns
On their way to somewhere and nowhere

I was Raised on Pearl Buttons

By Joan Audette

I was raised on pearl buttons
From the factory in town
Where my father labored
Amidst the deafening sound

Mother of Pearl shells
Imported from afar
Filled the large wooden crates
Stacked upon the floor

My father cut out circles
And these were called "blanks"
Using a thunderous machine
With the loudest of clanks

These pearly round discs
Were polished to a shine
Shipped to another site
Further down the line

At this destination
Punched with two holes or four
They gained a new name
They were not "blanks" anymore

I was raised on pearl buttons
For nineteen years, near a score
They provided the clothes
My siblings and I wore

Those pearl buttons bought chickens
For eggs and for meat
Bought seeds for the garden
Fresh vegetables to eat

They bought books and toys

And automobiles, too
For long Sunday drives
To admire the view

I was raised on pearl buttons
Oh those machines did sing!
I was raised on pearl buttons
It was a wonderful thing

In the Night

By Donna Smith

It comes in the night, it grabs you and bites,
Frozen in terror, body rigid with fright.
Frenzy and fear, ringing in your ear,
All semblance of calm evaporates and disappears.
Envelopes you whole, gripping your soul,
Feels like you're drowning with no control.
Sense of darkness and despair filling the air,
Body gripped in dread, too much to bear.
Images flashing in your eye, they flit and fly,
In horror and alarm, you let out a piercing cry.
Now in a panic, thoughts sporadic and manic,
Pouring and seeping out fast as if volcanic.
That feeling of foreboding, comes without a warning,
Mind filled with darkness longing for the morning.
And as you rise, you're really none to the wise,
Images disperse as you see with fresh eyes.
No longer in reach, your convictions now impeach,
Vanished, gone as if they've been bleached.
The more you awake, the dark thoughts you can shake,
A new dawn, a new day is here for you to take.

I Am Your Confessions

By Peter William Levi

Observing the human facade,
Everything hated deep within,
The things about themselves,
They attack with brutal wrath,
So call me whatever you will,
I'll wear their villainous crown,
As demonic confessions spill,
It's okay tho, because I can love,
The darkness that's in Everything,
Everyone, and every positive action,
You see, most humans ignore these,
Darker elements of themselves, and,
Explode anger towards what they're
Believing to be, that part of self that
Is not faceable. So call me by your
True name, call me, with anger in
Your heart. Let me, help you,
I'm the public enemy,
The Confessions,

Of You.

Cast with Fire

By Carmen Megiddo

A bird upon the wire inspired
Blue it was, and cast with fire
The bird looked down so haughtily
Fed on my soul's fresh ecstasy

Light was his image in my time,
Expectant of a lover's rhyme
The bird flew off to other climes
Behold, in him—the joys of time

Witness

By R. David Fletcher

Spirit tested to the breaking point,
In the devastation, fear and pain,
Creation delivers the tortured soul,
From the despot's death-soaked rain.

The courage that defies the suffering,
In the horror of their world,
Shines a light on hope and redemption,
In the travesty it unfurls.

Oh to be a Boat

By Sarah Tillbrook

Oh to be a boat
To be a boat out at sea
Rockin to the har'ch shore.

To the har'ch shore and back
Oh to see the wonders
Mermaids, treasured company.

Fast upon the waves
Set the course. Follow track.

Oh to feel the splish
As we glide past harbours ride
Stealing solar sunsets
Rays of hope past closured dawn.

Oh to sail away, sail a little farther pass' our side
Rocking on that rollin sea,
Morn to night, then night through morn.

Unforgettable

By Nan DeNoyer

It was such an enchanting night.
She was bathed in moonlight.
They had danced on to the balcony.
Ethereal was the moment almost a fantasy.
I noticed as we had embraced
how breathtakingly lovely her face.
Her scent wrapped itself around me.
Gently she moved even closer to be
near my face, her breath I could feel.
She became unable to conceal
as her emotions were stirred.
I whispered softly, I heard
a sigh, she trembled a bit.
We succumbed to the ambiance I admit.
Had she bewitched me?
Her lips parted slightly
as if waiting to be kissed.
I was unable to resist
a tender moment like this.

My Words

By Donna Smith

You may read, then critique, my speak,
Voice your view, sharp opinion too.
It doesn't rhyme,
Beat not in time.
It lacks vision,
Lacks pace,
Words written down in haste.
Missing a tau,
Missing a tittle,
You can try to belittle,
My words,
My work,

Punctuation and grammar,
It may seem,
Is second rate, shoddy, spelling,
Also deemed,
Substandard and shocking.

But,
I
Don't
Really care,
If you declare,
I shouldn't share.

And
I
Remain neutral,
If you think,
My poetry is futile.

They are my words,
My sentences,
To own.
My passion,
To express,
I don't write to impress,
You,
Or anyone else,
But to release,
The emotions I feel,
To enable me to relax and heal.
To laugh, to lighten,
My sense heightened.
To cry, to chaff,
At this world,
And all that is absurd.
To write about all that is great and good,
All that bring us joy and great sadness,
And all that lies in between.
Through free verse and satire,
It is my heart's desire.

Very Convincing

By Leelah Saachi

I challenge you to find me I said,
Behind whatever disguises I offer!
I will find you, he said, even if you hide
In the crack between centuries.

I turned myself into a deserted
Garden, rusty iron fence with croaking
Hinges, whining and complaining at
Human touch. Dry and brown spotted

Leaves on the ground, cracked flagstones
With tired yellow grass

I filled the sad house with mould and cold,
Dust and rust, and hid my heart in the cellar.
My disguise was so convincing that I
Disappeared into it, I became the deserted
House with coleoptera, spider webs as curtains,
I forgot it was a game

For aeons I forgot
Then - one day the sky was filled with pink
Like a bedsheet of happiness drawn all up to one's nose
And you sun rained into my creation!
You met me in the cellar stairs
And grinned
And I remembered that I thought I could be lost!
How did you recognize me, I asked
And you just shook your head at such
A silly question
My heart burst out in daffodils
We frolicked for quite a while
And then I wanted to play hide again
Since it is feels so darn good to be found
and seen through

Dissolving

By Leelah Saachi

As the pixels melted together
in a soup of zeroes and ones
mixed with tiny bits of amoebas
and dinosaurs,

I turned to my husband and said,
The web is going, dear.
He looked at the screen and nodded twice,
His director-eyes gazing into
stage designs not yet created.
"Shakespeare knew this.
The world is a dream, and
we are all being dreamed
And now the curtain falls."
We watched as the screen dissolved

Outside the large windows
The spruces had moved closer, emerald green
Fragrant and filled with grace
The duck pond swelled with pleasure
A red fox stood still
His tail quivering
I watched as the walls dissolved

The skies were alive with blue and orange birds
They screamed and circled our home
As I watched my left thumb dissolve

My beloved took me in his arms and
smiled and said with tremendous basso-profundo voice,
"It will all go, my love, the Dreamer is waking up."
He kissed me and we dissolved

Nobody watched

Steam Train

By Lee Smith

Shhhhhush and a whirling squeal
As the wheels grip the rail
Edging gently forward like a giant snail
With a gentle clatter from carriages behind
Then a clickety clack as they go down the line
Building up speed with a billow of smoke
Carriages bursting with holiday folk
Fireman feeding fire shovelling coal
Brass shining bright like shimmering gold
Stood on the footplate the driver observes
The pitch of the hill and the depth of the curves
Pulls on the whistle as crossings we pass
Full steam ahead travelling fast

The World is Upside Down

By Victoria Puckering

The world is upside down
Wrong way around
I am lost
I am found
That poetic sound rings in my ear
Piercing
They sing to me
The words find a way through
To me
To you
The words are black and white
Moving quick
I do not have time to think
My hand just writes this flow of words
Conducted by the pain
Words and pain flowing to my hurting brain
No time to think
Spontaneous ink

Overwhelmed with too much pain
Poetry my distraction
The world is upside down
Wrong way around
I am lost
I am found

I am found
I am lost
Wrong way around
The world is upside down
Poetry my distraction
Overwhelmed with too much pain
Spontaneous ink
No time to think
Words and pain flowing to my hurting brain
Conducted by the pain
My hand just writes this flow of words
I do not have time to think
Moving quick
The words are black and white
To you
To me
The words find a way through
They sing to me
Piercing
That poetic sound rings in my ear
I am found
I am lost
Wrong way around
The world is upside down

I Have A Dream

By Kalucharan Sahu

I have a dream!
A dream where there will be no tomorrow
While I row a boat, leaving a trail of furrow.
On the resplendent waters, sparkling

Under the benevolent moon, flooding
The dour earth with its heavenly light .
My beautiful and favorable sight.

I have a dream!
Of people frolicking on the sands,
Where children build castles and grandstands,
While the soft waves splash and swish
The structures before the children could finish.

I have a dream!
Of people living without boundaries
Made by men, jovial and full of camaraderie;
A canvas of kaleidoscopic creation,
Painted with love, ardour and passion.

I have a dream!
I know too short is the night
For my dream to take flight;
But dream I will without rest
Till they take wings and crest.

Visited the Gone Era

By Shafkat Aziz

Visited the gone era by turning the pages,
Knew about the life of saints and sages
Accompanied by them for a while,
Found them, to their Lord, entirely loyal.
Of gone era, turned the pages of my land,
Found each one a helping hand,
Generous and kind without envy
Such humour today we rarely see.
Visited the families, found them gay,
Venerating the elders, adoring the young,
Living their days without fray.
And found them walking hand in hand,
Ascending every rung of the ladder of their life,
Without greed and enmity,
resolving their differences without a strife.

The Sunrise

By Kalucharan Sahu

The night smoulders sensuously from its deep sleep,
The time has come to rise, for it has a date to keep,
The long wait has ended, and the resplendent Sun is at the door
Swishing off the night's darkness with its shiny robes of splendor.

The first rays held the night under its grasp,
making it swell in delight,
The night blushed coyly and turned red and amber
and played with light.
It melted like ice, bit by bit, and dissolved itself
in the arms of the Sun
As the mist, the fog and the darkness disappeared in the horizon.

The warmth of the Sun seeped everywhere, and the birds flew
Fluttering their feathers, shaking off in glee the morning dew.
The sheets of white light splashed across the body of the night;
The stars felt cheated and shut themselves off from sight.

A new dawn, a new beginning, a renewal of life,
and a chain of spectacles;
The Sunrise spreads over hills and dales,
reviving our faith in miracles.

Memorial (to life)

By Sarah Tillbrook

The river paused
For no-one
The fish swam
Inhuman
The dogs called
In packs
The sun hit their backs
A something
It was coming
The beasts

They came a thrumming
Until the river
Paused
Are we fighting
A lost cause!?
Solar flares
And heating systems
Oil churns
Without resistance
We're avoiding
Renewable power
And so dies
That wilting flower
And the fish
The dogs, the water
They're disappearing
And though we oughta...
We don't remember
A river ran
First a river
What's next? Man?

Crested Wave

By Mark Edward Dickinson

When your light can no longer shine
Through the darkness bound in the night
Be the crested wave that aligns
and reflects off another's light.

Heed not the call of its brother
From the depths of the trough it shouts
to stifle the lights of others
so its darkness is known throughout

Rage, against that which calls to thee
The calls to steal another's light
For they want not the world to see
The emptiness that fills their night.

Napalm Clouds

By Tony Dukeva

Beyond the pastures once prolific
There is a prospect most horrific
An urban desert wrapped in fog
Impending napalm clouds convoke.

The vigour of the raid's obsessive
And every next move – more aggressive
In dust and dirt, the buildings droop
The remnants float in bloody soup.

Remote the people don't look back
Defect the imminent attack
The wind, offended, only stares
At that lacuna blank and bare.

The Side Door

By Imelda Zapata Garcia

as you walk in past the vestíbule
behind that side door entrance
the elegant Baby Grand, you view
there is a feeling of repentance

a sense, too overwhelming to ignore
generations, can't erase looming dread
you've entered through the help's door
the door which only they used instead

this once Southern mansion of a house
which at that time, could not do without
the help to tend the drapes and the spouse
of the ever present master, roaming about

though battered by time to less grand
holds yet a tale tell, with a side door
meant to hide the mere helping hands
screams its sordid past, as before

I Can Hear Granny

By Joan Audette

The empty porch swing sways silently in the summer breeze
But I can hear Granny, singing
and shelling peas
Granny in her apron, braided hair atop her head
Socks drooping over those old creased shoes
Over the well-worn path on the old porch floor
Rocking to and fro, fro and to
I hear the crow of long gone roosters
The lowing of ghost cows in the pastures green
The pinging of the peas into the old metal pan
The one that had lost its sheen
I see the faded red barn; the un-mown fields
And before my eyes, disappear the years
For there is Granny in the porch swing
Swaying in the summer breeze
I can hear her softly singing and shelling those peas
Ping ping ping
Ping ping
Ping

Legacy

By R. David Fletcher

I suppose I've given them memories,
These children life calls mine;
Wind-swept shores and emerald lake,
The laughter of ebbing time.

There's nothing here to teach you, child
But the gift of life anew;
Take the road that gives you light,
For the years they are so few.

And so, they came to know

By Pureheart Wolf

What are your dreams?
A life made with tarnished sequins
The string that holds us together
Binding of beads, that became untethered

Secrets held deep
There, be no bleating from sheep,
Only the sound of silence
With words of defeat

Did your courage keep you strong?
Did the beads drop one by one?
Each pearl a broken song,
It's time for moving on.

Impossible

By Tony Dukeva

Among the things people desire
There is one thing that I admire
Impossible as it may seem
Provokes in my soul ice and steam.
To turn back time—this I conspire
And I can't pacify myself from all that fire
That I don't have a second chance
To dream, to smile, to dance again
Among those years of my youth
When my soul was so bright and smooth
And now is kept on a metal leash
From all fatigue there is no release
But liquid drops of sadness carving
Representation of suspension
And all restraints from this dimension
give me no reasonable comprehension.

Depression's Abrupt Wall

By Suzanne Newman

My goodness...who turned out the light?!
A minute ago I was feeling alright,
But now it seems my head has turned,
And it aches and hurts where the darkness burns.

I was doing fine, and then suddenly
Depression slams a wall in front of me,
From nowhere, there's a barrier made of brick,
One hundred miles long and twenty feet thick.

This debilitating, cold, cruel wall
Looms at ten thousand meters tall,
No light can pass this harsh, bleak black,
There is no give and no hint of a crack.

I don't know how these icy bricks
Made a solid impasse quite so quick,
In what seemed like five minutes flat,
My mind's switched into midnight black.

I reach out, just to feel the stones,
Which numb and chill and make me groan,
The coldness really zaps my strength,
Makes heart hang low and shoulders tense.

Depression knows it's a frightening foe,
Takes pleasure in pain and cultivates sorrow,
It's a worry to find I can't see past
This black shield and the despair which lasts.

It's hard to live where there is no light,
The future's grim...anything but bright,
The shadow cast by depression's wall
Consumes joy to make peace and hope grow small.

I feel so cold and all alone,
Mind's squashed and squeezed by slabs of stone,
Which hem me in so mercilessly,
'til thoughts aren't mine and brain's not free.

I panic and cede and sink to my knees,
Depression is winning…it's gloating and pleased,
But, when I've no hope, The Lord provides some,
Throws me a life-line, when my own's come undone.

Lord Jesus stands by me and is here all the while,
He summons my strength, gives peace reason to smile,
He tells me to sit tight and exercise faith,
Reassures me He'll help, in His unfailing grace.

What I lose to depression, God will turn to my gain,
Perseverance will thrive and my faith grows in pain,
The Lord does ensure when depression attacks
My soul remains safe and untouched by the black.

Soul's bravery's contagious and helps keep me going
Throughout all life's struggles and when cold winds blow in,
So, I won't give up, nor give in to this trial,
For The Lord walks this wall with me…each troubled mile.

And, one day, I trust that I'll come to the end
Of depression's dark wall and then my mind will mend,
Until then, I'll just have to ignore all the tricks
That depression does play, with its nightmarish bricks.

I Will Sing, I Will Dance...

By Aaron Blackie

I sat on the clear
Open field, saxophone
Before my lips,
Ready to sing the song
Out of the depths
Where pure rhythms lie...

Then the falcon
Came by saying, sing now
A song for me instead;
The song of the watchman
The rodents, the pesterer
Creatures, I have hunted out
Of your home space

Oh, watchman of the
Home front, how can I sing you
A song, amid spilled
Blood, marking the landmarks
To my fluffy home?

The falcon flew on,
The sunny voice of the hummingbird
Nearby flowers, caught
My melodiously inclined soul..
Sing for me instead,
The melody of flowery beauty!

Yes, I love to sing
you a song, oh sustainer of alluring
Roses, that it's all glowing
Here, but time changes, the wind
Blows, roses falloff,
Beauty fades, not keeping
Long to its glows...

Lifted my eyes

To the rooftop, its soulful voice
Singing in a titillating tune...
The dove, the symbol of what its
Conveys: peace and
Tranquillity, beckons on me, join
In the synchronizing
Flow, spreading tunes of harmony,
A symbiotic rhythms
In the air and hope reawakened!

I am the astute soprano
Saxophonist. You are the soulful
Tenor. Let the
Clapping leaves, fill the space
Of our scintillating dance steps!

Flowering Floor

By Imelda Zapata Garcia

The very first house my parents bought
shiny door knobs shone the new hue
everything in the place, where it ought
fresh coat of paint, proved how new

we took pride in the appearance of it
kept everything as clean as we could
windows, so clear it made others covet
the pristine house, made of wooden

the first time I mopped, there was in store
caught side of a glimmer of gold
yellow bud growing in a crack on the floor
how was it possible, it was months old

on the seam where floor tiles met
a hearty dandelion sprouted tall
quite baffling a treat, you can bet
a strange occurrence to one and all

Don't Storm Out on a Gentle Night

By Jimmy Ray Davis

Well I'm not sure why you read my ramblings,
if you're bored, I can't tell.
We may never meet at the crossroads
but I'll surely
see you in hell.
When you cry a thousand tears
then wipe them dry.
You'll wonder but never figure out
the reason why.
If wings don't rip from your shoulders
you will never fly.
Just don't storm out on a gentle night.

For your ship has once again run aground.
Oceans of emotion in your sea.
I may not share all of my secrets
but we can sit,
and have some tea.
When you scream in the night
for someone to love,
there will be no light from
the sky above.
Maybe all you need is just
a little shove.
Just don't storm out on a gentle night.

I'm sitting in my car outside the SpeakEasy.
Her voice soothes, all the rage.
No matter what rhymes I choose to spew.
Will I ever
turn that page?
Sunny words come from, skies of grey
Poets never die, they just fade away.
If you're gonna leave

maybe you should stay.

Just don't storm out on a gentle night.

Leaves of your life will often crumble.
Brown with age, broken shells.
Down that ragged hill you must tumble
if you ever want to reach
that wishing well.
I can wrap you in my strong arms
and try to explain.
Just because you feel crazy doesn't mean
that you're insane.
You can depart at the next stop or keep
riding that train.
Just don't storm out on a gentle night.

In Low Spirits

By Khursheed Wani

On people's minds, lasting
The agony of a year ago
Fell I from sight
Away from the heart.

A wave offensive, came
Wiped out my amour propre,
What an irony?
It may last a lifetime.

Living in it, a living hell
All efforts went in vain,
I lost my native wit,
Sombre! I broke the reveries.

Just the eyes saw a nightmare,
Scary scenes in the crepuscule,
It came inside me like a storm,
I sighed, I cried, I swamped in despair.

Silence

By Promise Speedii

Heart keeps aching
Body keeps shaking
For those thoughts are kept hidden
A mysterious garden
Those words I wish to say
But would remain a story in my heart
Cause I don't want to stab myself
with the reality I would face
By saying words I wished you could listen to
But then the silence keeps hurting
More and more each day
Only If I know you could care
About those words of mine
Just maybe this silence wouldn't hurt so badly

This Time, Our Time

By Carol A. Turni

The strangeness of these days,
Life disrupted and different.
The danger of these days,
Shots fired and lives finished.
The constant change of these days,
Our rights, restricted and wrecked.
The fear of these days,
Forever changed and full of chaos.
The sadness of these days,
Spiralling depression and desperation.

Everything seems hard. It is hard.

These times call for our truths,
Not our conformity and concessions.
These times call for our voices,
Not our silence and suppression.

These times call for our hearts to open,
Allowing both empathy and sympathy.
These times call for real conversations,
Allowing for opinions without oppression.
These times call for our common humanity,
Connecting our oneness and sameness.

A call to love more, not love less.
This is our time.

State of Mind

By Carol A. Turni

I stumbled away from sanity
Into the arms of chaos
Fighting the good fight
Emotionally at a loss

Trying to catch my breath
In a race against time
Carving out my path
Keeping step with mankind

Our future quite unknown
Leaves my mind blown
Will we see the other side?
Or our future denied

I fear the end is in sight
Directionless thoughts
Leads to confusion
Is this real or an illusion?

Our reality is up for grabs
Stability is not common
Is our future clearly seen
Is it a nightmare or a weird dream?

Old Oak Door

By Carol A. Turni

At the end of the hall,
Stands an old oak door.
Held closed by an iron gate,
Yes, the one of ancient folklore.

Dare to open that sturdy door,
Amazed at what you might find.
A place lost not so long ago,
Mind's open space, lost in past times.

A place of your long ago dreams,
And innocence of a lifetime past.
A place of locked away thoughts,
Of connections that did not last.

Not very many get beyond that gate.
More so now, with all the covert hate.
Shadows seen peeping thru the hole,
Their faces I no longer recognize or know.

That gated, old Oak Door.
Tall, strong, steady and stable.
Faces and dreams that reappear,
My eye sheds a tear, maybe next year.

The Collective

By Imelda Zapata Garcia

this entity grows casting off
only the souls
swallows humanity, moves
to control
our genius dripping from its nose
it spins our senses
into gears which turn

mechanical, artificial intelligence
is its form
piled on armour, hides
its nature cold
appearing sentient with
traces of skin
adorned from head
to claw foot toes
our skulls hanging
from high and low
hoarding, collecting
to be made whole
stealing our hearts
with ritual force
leaving all, vulnerable, open
exposed to assimilation
as we become the very hull
of it, who claims to be
the collective

The Lighthouse

By Pureheart Wolf

Meet me by the lighthouse
Beacon shining bright
Reflections on the water
Two lovers' hearts ignite
A love that was forbidden
From different walks of life
They would meet beside the lighthouse
A lover's quest delight
They swore to one another
They would marry there one day
Beside the tall white lighthouse
Their bodies entwined with play
Then one day his love was followed
Her Father had his say
His daughter will not marry

His word "They will obey!"
Both planned to meet in secret
It would be their very last
Her Father had a shotgun
And fired two mighty blasts
Now lovers, haunt the lighthouse
They wander round at night
You may see them by the water
Apparitions shining bright.

the colored number of my counted days

By Matthew Elmore

refresh me within your sight blameless
painless ageless the bounty of harvest
wash over the pain that haunts this jest

worldly ghost peeping through walls
into my eyes leave without drama please
redemption relentless define my times

rainbow of remembrance bestow your rays
upon the colored number of my counted days

–

embellish an answer of a quest impressed
weightless stainless upon the vistas crest
imply the mystery invested in this test

intentional fortitude strengthen my heart
captain a ship sailing never found failing
of excessive blessing refine now my mind

shadows of regret surrender your shade
into the vibrant sunshine of love I have made

–

summarize the tide once denied depressed
oppressed obsessed with being the best
allow me the most by becoming the less

wisdom profound befriend this mad beast
grant me peace and assure my release
surrendered senseless to design the sublime

release my faulty secrets residing internal
into a resolution now thankful and eternal

Motherlode

By Carmen Megiddo

Upon the mural of my soul I see the prize
Set forth as alien to an alien face;
Imprinted is an angel of a trusting grace—
Formed by the heavenly flattery of his eyes.

I fix my jaded eyes upon this glowering man
Shining in perfect converse with his guile;
I keep my rosy gaze upon his subtle smile,
And bring the sign of my ingenious plan.

I am the queen that comes in terrible disguise,
Even through the ashes of a mournful pyre
Reason, memory and wine I so desire,
Gazing on the fateful vision formed within his eyes.

We stand like pyramids beneath the motherlode;
Turned as a memory of the shadows in the west;
Vexed by that heavenly flattery for their rest,
We see the burning stars strewn 'cross our road.

Words by Proxy

By John Rennie

It's never easy or nice
when you lose a friend
cruel words said in spite
unfeeling messages sent
the tide can't be turned back
just ask Canute about that
it always ebbs and flows
not all friendships grow
what's said is said and
what's done is sadly done
arguments will always be lost
disagreements are never won
words said in remote form
screaming out loud by proxy
everything is overblown
it all becomes so toxic
for myself, I can only apologise
but the rest is up to you
I can only see it through my eyes
who really knows the truth?
I wish you well, my friend
never meant to cut you down
all good things come to an end.
in the end, I guess we're clowns
I always valued you, my friend
guess I didn't tell you enough
every road and journey has an end
and the getting there is tough.
I wish you well, my friend.

Nyra

By Genevieve Ray

Nyra;
Autumn born.
Kitsune of the hopeless,
drawing an oblong demi goddess.
By the creases of your smile.

Nyra;
My starlight rose.
You awoke my sleeping Sappho.
You tender strength,
sliced my woven bonds.

Nyra;
wandering enchantress.
A mothering vixen,
Whose emerald gaze,
disperses storms.

Nyra;
watercolour heart.
From pages you called me,
opened up desire,
to transverse new galaxies.

Nyra;
Venus, revisited.
Hathor of the open road.
Your story ends in mystery,
And poly romantic melody.
New deity of the starlight highway.

Footprint
By Fiona Halliday

The footprint of a baby,
Immortalised in plaster.
The footprint of an astronaut,
Made history for humankind.
The footprint of a dinosaur,
Undiscovered for many millennia.
The footprint of a soldier,
On unforgiving ground.
The footprint of a faithful one,
Helping others to believe.
The footprint of the hopeless,
Standing at a grave.
The footprint of our wastage,
Upon our Earth so green.
The footprint of the broken hearts,
The world has never seen.

Black Canvas
By Ashley O'Keefe

Flying in
On feathered wings,
An artist's brush strokes
A blackbird sings,
Within a dream
A rosy glow,
Lights up the darkness
Gently rivers flow,
A pure black canvas
Now burning bright,
Colours my world
Brings forth new sight,
Warm summer days
Amongst fields of hay,
Here comes the dawn
A brand-new day.

Corpse

By Marten Hoyle

What have I to say or fear?
The loneliness of tomorrow
Sounds like Heaven:
The silence I dare not face
Must feel so lovely.

Untouched by sorrow
As I stare at the tomb.
I can't remember who lies there.
Surely, they must have been beautiful—
Never have I seen a grave half so fair.

"Let's become snow,"
I whisper to the sleeper.
"We shall freeze the flowers,
And the bluebirds shall sing
Over a blossomless bed."
But I heard no answer
From the jewelled dead.

The sky is wilting amid the leaves.
What have we to fear?
The loneliness that is to come
Shall repulse the spirits of Once Upon a Time—
The memories when laughter unfolded of old.
Or do I remember nothing?
The memory is clear. But is it mine?

Whose mind do I share?
Yesterday is a haunted place...
But were we there among those solitary ages?
I seem to remember nothingness of what came before,
And I view the nothingness that is to come.
You know of it well, dear corpse,
And you speak nothing of what it is.
I fear I have lost the spaces between then,

And what will not be.
And when I ask of you what will come
You do not answer me.

"Let us become sunlight,"
I say to the sleeper.
We shall bring the flowers to bloom,
And the butterflies shall sing over the roses.
But no answer rises from the tomb.

Sunset

By Rob Bristol

As the sunlight fades away,
Preparing for a brand new day,
Night time spreads her wings of dark,
Lovers strolling in the park.

Stars which twinkle in the sky,
Reflect upon the human eye,
The moon emerges from the gloom,
Creating shadows in my room.

The wise old owl takes to flight,
Hunting through the darkened night,
Bats awaken from their sleep,
In dense forests, creatures creep.

Upon deep oceans, ships sail by,
Accompanied by a seagulls cry,
Passing silent on the waves,
Pirates rest in unmarked graves.

Lovers strolling in the park,
Night time spreads her wings of dark,
Preparing for a brand new day,
As the sunlight fades away...

Fireflies

By Marten Hoyle

I feel so profoundly disturbed
When I see the rain pouring down
In the sunlight where I am alone
On a walk through the cemetery.
I hear the silent graves weeping
With voices that may be my own.
Am I dying, or have I gone insane?
I hear them say I've been talking to myself,
And they all are laughing at the way I look
In such company as I walk along the green.

I never saw the fireflies they mentioned.
But there are shadows in my field,
A deeper dark in the depths of coming night,
Where they say I'll see those men with their needles
When my mind dies in the glow of the fireflies…

I wonder if I'll see the moon through my windowpane
When I've lost my way home among the ghosts again.
My love is fading, and I do not know if it's something I can save.
I want to make the sunshine, but the night is deep,
As I sail through the rain to the border of some far-off country
Where voices have lost their way.
No matter how I try to hear them, I cannot extinguish
The glow of what the dead said were the fireflies
In the needles who speak so softly
Of a place where I may rest within the hours of the hills:

Just watch the hills…
To the hills, it will be but a moment…

Waking in the haze of your traces
With the scent of death upon my lips—
I wonder…will you fade as everything else?
Are you an image, or are you the same?
I do not know what exists…I do not know…
There is a presence beside me….
But when I turn to face it
There is only light…the light of the fireflies.

This is Where We Lose

By Abril Garcia Linn

I wrap my arms around my daughter's thin waist
and squeeze
rest my nose against her head
inhale the almond scent of oil in her hair
and cry

I sit quietly with my son in our car
hold his heavy hand in mine
look into his worried eyes
and cry

I cry for the mothers and fathers
that will no longer savor the sweet scent of their babies
I cry for the babies that are ripped from their loving arms
I cry for our children living in terror
who survived a deadly pandemic
emerged from isolation into a world so broken
and beholden to greed

This is where we lose

I watch our children talk
laugh and play
go about their day
numb to the stories of carnage
accustom to the horror
expecting us
their elders
to keep them safe

But we are in shock
filled with grief
still processing our collective trauma
another mass shooting headlines
and the cycle will not end
if we stay silent

Let us cry together
Let us scream at the tops of our lungs
Let us fall apart   together
and then let us gently wipe each other's tears
Hold each other's hands
and fight
to end this nightmare

This is where we win

Perennial as the Grass

By Shirley Cruz

I find splendid beauty
In your verdant lushing leaves
Your flowers swiftly sway
So pleasant to my eyes;
In some season,
You seem to fade
Your leaves have withered
Totally covered by flood
Your roots strongly hold
on the fertile soil
At some time,
You sprout again
You grow majestically
Thriving and dancing
In summer or in rain;
Hope and strength,
You remind of man
Amid nature's wrath
or life's adversities,
Man remains steadfast
Like the perennial grass.

Perspective

By Julie Sheldon

How tiny they seem from my garden
Those aeroplanes flying up high
It's hard to believe there are people
Sat inside a tube in the sky
What do they see from those small windows?
A patchwork of towns, roads and fields?
Do they think of me far below them?
Whilst savouring their in-flight meals

My phone has a smart application
So I can track each single flight
I hear them before I can see them
The evening sun sets them alight
I wait for the next set of travellers
I look to the clouds passing by
The sun, sinking on the horizon
Casts turquoise and pink through the sky

As night falls, the stars make their entrance
They twinkle so tiny and bright
The moon starts to shine on its crescent
Delivering light to the night
Perhaps I will see a star shooting
Or satellites circling up high
I may even see the space station
I'll wave to the crew passing by

How different things look from new angles
But sometimes we just cannot see
We get so weighed down with life's problems
We can't see the wood for the tree
We're full of our own self importance
All wrapped up in everyday life
Try putting things into perspective
Start looking up into the sky

Master He Arose

By James C. Little

Those humble hearts who amply live
to fill their hoards with modest gems,
finely sing like cherubim.
Good sense as universal as the faith
in God's great plan shall sure proceed,
is common to their breed.
They fix their foods to honest be,
yes, nourish flesh, not vanity:
no pretty picture on a page,
or any work of artistry.

They make their suits of denim twill
twice wove by lively weavers
in a sturdy purple thread,
bolstered by the homespun love
that bids our souls be still.

These plain true hearts
quite merry make when work's
complete here in His Will.
They thrill to fill themselves
with Angel cake, to breathe on Truth,
that which He spake.

Fix well thy soul upon His star
to practice piety at home;
to know that virtue covers those
who plain and simple be,
who know that, yes, my Master He arose:
And from that knowledge never roam.

The Eyes of Love

By Shirley Cahayom

The eyes of love stare at me
bright and intense as the desert sun
I see in you the newly-awakened dawn
its garment spread in phosphorescent rays
that envelop my naked soul, keeping it warm
like the rich Colombian brew.
through the years, I keep you safely
tucked in my heart, nurturing you
through the center of my being. I bask in your periwinkle days
that tango with the wind and bear the pain and loneliness
of the aubergine nights of despair that cripple my soul
and shatter it into a thousand and one microscopic pieces
that takes another heart to mend. But the moon is always there
filtering through the window pane. Its luminescence lulls me
to golden slumber where I can chase my multi-colored dreams.

Never Again

By Bhoj Kumar Dhamala

Exquisite,
Immaculate, and gracious
Your presence in this exclusive world
Has some purpose, fulfilled with the supreme fragrance.

Wanton
Down in a blooming garden
Morning dew, a crystal, drops downwards
The life splashes inside, waiting for the twilight.

Proliferate,
Craft and create unfading life,
Like the early morning with no clouds of vagueness,
As you overlook, never again you get a chance of
redemption.

The Tutelage of the Wind

By Aaron Blackie

I grew vulnerable to cold trap,
Wintry winds beaten on my
Skinny skin... Helpless, often, I winced!
Come close, son of my supple
Delights...I will give you warm milk
Originated from the
Suckled breasts of my nine
Months of tearful joy!
Warmly shielded with weather-proven
Body, all day long, mother comforted
But sooner than expected, dust
Returned to the home of dusts,
Plunging me swiftly into the abyss
Of cuddled voidness:
The tutelage of the wind!

He braced through
The hurdles of life along weaves
Of labyrinths on the pathways.
Snatches of wisdom for
Living along the torturous journeys,
He gathered into the barns of reality...
Son, you are the seed
Protruded out of my loins, the
Flowering of my morning strength...
Follow this path I proffered,
Your days shall be shallow, not side-tracked.
Long gone, father, the road taken
Placed siege on my roaring talents:
The tutelage of the wind!

The God-man of our
Frenzied delights,
That could do no wrong...
He whetted our paths with seasoned
Wisdoms out of his dripping lips,
Cascading like sparkling waterfalls.

Can flesh and blood be so infallible
As to become the ultimate fountain
Of our vision and essence?
Soon a daring Jezebel became the
Shadow of his image;
The reference point of his great story:
The tutelage of the wind!

I will not give up on the
Flowery cultures of tutelage essence,
But hold strong to my rein:
For besides all known to us,
The mystery of the future largely dwells
In the ocean floor of indeterminacy
Yet the arrows of knowing,
Must constantly be sharpen and shoot
Onward, strides for the mazy paths ahead...

Heaven's Grand Marquee

By James C. Little

Forever joyful do our spirits be
when hope in silent rapture smiles
through miracles built end to end
and woven in a tapestry.
Forever dulcet do our rhythms be
when love in soothing pleasure
fulfils hearts laid chest to chest and
beating two in harmony.
Exhilarating thrills of turned-on life
induce emotions off the charts,
but far too sweet!
for feelings spawned in syrup impart
a love that flows too slow to give away,
and therefore clogs said hearts
in sad dismay.
Their senses fail, are blind but cannot braille
or learn the light of everyday,
or hear one's whispered tenderness

for lust that soon becomes satiety.
Their speech is harsh and painful to our ear,
and though it speaks out to be heard,
our highest pleasure is its doom, its noise interred.
Vile vocal spiel inverse to length cedes levity –
We'd sure appreciate more brevity.
But they who live their lives as poems
with beauty ever building be
the stars who fill God's skies,
on Heaven's Grand Marquee.
Forever joyful will our spirits be,
Your living kingdom come in me
and we are home
through miracles you built for us
embraced within your ecstasy.

Your True Colour

By Catherine A. MacKenzie

You pile the mortar upon me,
thickly,
in layers,
inch by inch,
as if you do it fast enough
you think I won't discover your games.
You think I won't escape.
And upon the mortar
you lay the bricks,
one at a time,
brick by brick,
and they attach to the mortar,
adhering for all time
you think,
until eventually they break free,
but the red of the brick
continually shows through
to reveal your true colour.

Faces
By Catherine A. MacKenzie

I look in the mirror
And what do I see?
The face of my mother
Staring back at me.
I glance at my daughter
A mother now too,
Her face familiar,
Ageing too fast.
I view my granddaughter,
Innocent and wee,
Alive on her face
A once-portrait of me.

Positive Difference
By Julie Sheldon

You cannot solve all the world's problems
You cannot bring wars to an end
You cannot heal everyone's heartache
Or cure the disease of a friend

You can try to make someone happy
You can share your love and goodwill
You can lend a hand where it's needed
To help someone climb up their hill

With each helping hand that you offer
With every kind gesture you make
If all of us work hard together
A positive difference we'll make

Grounded Home on a Courtyard

By Lawal Ibrahim Hibie

Here I errand, searching for a home
Where humanity has ever sought asylum till eternity –
Wearing every beat of my heart for survival;
Survival of the fittest in love
Love hates to like death
Death at the expense of the soul
Soul lives unrest in everybody
Everybody is a walking corpse – wandering –
Wandering around and across the earth
Earth mistaken as life
Life which is grounded as a home on a grave
Grave, where all things ended up –
Resurrected.

Fireflies and the Moon

By Marie Harris

Blowing bubbles under the gaze of a benevolent moon
While fireflies spread their diamond glint
As the moon's reflection is captured
Her magic upon my mind imprints

Pure and sweet the moment
Like a painting on a moving screen
Purple and mauve is the evening shade
Dotted with fireflies in between

A dalliance with delight
As the night does so softly enfold
My mind is awash in the beauteous veil of peace
As I am held in awe by the fairy tale ambience I behold

The dusk of this magic summer evening
Gives over to the consuming velvet ebony of the night
Leaving my mind with enchantment etched
By the magic I was part of on this evening of delight

Paint and Shadows

By Catherine A. MacKenzie

The painted portrait coloured
by wedded bliss
hangs upon a small hook,
decorating the wall,
eyes stare into a future
that will hold memories.
Two faces,
young and fresh and innocent,
with hopes and dreams
and plans and goals
share their past
and now their future
and fortune
together as one.
Sixty years later
another portrait hangs in its stead,
images of lines and shadows
drawn from years of living
and wedded bliss,
framed by the glow of
burning candles,
a shadow of two lives
living together as one.
And then there is only one life left,
alone,
the cord cut
and breath stopped
amid precious rain,
memories of a life
lived with another,
and one doesn't forget
while watching from above,
blowing love in the breeze
and hiding kisses
in the raindrops,
expressions of wonderful
wedded bliss.

Two framed portraits
now united as one love,
forever and ever,
eyes watching still,
encompassing all,
hang above the mantle
upon small hooks,
two old souls' hushed voices
in the night,
dulled by the flame
and reunited once more in love,
kissed by raindrops
and caressed by autumn leaves
falling upon the concrete slab.

Rare Flowers

By Rhiannon Owens

You will be mine, just as I will be yours,
I called mutely across the distance,
until my silent throat was hoarse...

I remonstrated with my feelings,
tried to cast you from my mind,
but it was my heart where you resided,
so you were never hard to find...

I felt sad at night, thinking of you—
it was worse in those early hours,
yet by day those thoughts left in their wake
a trail of vibrant flowers...

As bright and hopeful as a love
that took us by surprise,
as rare and beautiful as those emotions
sparkling in our eyes...

Chasing the Light

By Ashley O'Keefe

It's a long Winter's road
Into the setting sun,
Chasing the light
Slowly coming undone,

Darkness is falling
Spreading across the land,
Those skeletal shadows
Made from a skeletal hand,

A cold moon whitens
The ice-covered ground,
In silhouette, the trees
Stripped bare, make no sound.

Words

By Naomi G. Tangonan

with (more or less)
mixed feelings
here i express
the love i have for you
since i learned my
alphabets and i saw
the magic you can do
you captivated me
like no other
enchanted me like the
tales of long ago
fairies princes princesses
knights in shining armors
spears and arrows
horses and chariots
i devoured books like

a hungry lion takes his prey
i was your slave your wish
is my command always at your
bidding in the middle of night
or daybreak and high noon
twilight in the setting sun
you give me life
you give me power you
give meaning to everything
i think say do or feel
you've never left me nor
forsaken me
you are all i really have
you are mine and i am yours
what would my life be
without you
words!

The Empty Room

By Martin Pickard

The weekly wash is smaller than before
The food shop half the size it used to be
No bathroom towels in piles upon the floor
and breakfast tray holds just two cups of tea
Her room now echoes with a mother's sighs
With longing for her daughter to appear.
The tiny tears that fell from dolly's eyes
The carpet stains from games of yesteryear
Now she lives in a new house of her own
The one they saved so many years to buy
And pieces of the nest that she has flown
Now decorate their lovers' sanctuary
My body fills with pride as I observe
My princess in the palace she deserves

If I Were a Poet

By David Arndt

If I were a poet
My words
Would say
What lives
In my heart
But is hidden
Away
If I were a poet
My words
Would swoon
Color the sky
And light up
The moon
If I were a poet
My words
Would play
Invite you
Home
Never send
You away
If I were a poet
My words
Would soar
Give you
The Key
To unlock my
Heart's door
If I were a poet
My words
Would dream
Take you away
To hidden worlds
That have
Never been
Seen
If I were a poet
My words

Would touch you
You would
Feel my love
And never
Be blue
If I were a poet
My words
Would bring
Love
To all living
Creatures
Below and
Above
If I were a poet
My words
Would shine bright
They would
Tuck you in bed
And kiss you
Goodnight

Through Stone

By Jesse Batista

I want to disappear
To no particular place
Away from the clamor and the chaos
Where no one knows my face
To a corner of the world
Where the mountains reach the sky
Where there's a quiet in the breeze
On which majestic eagles fly
Pink and yellow sapphire
Embellish the blue
The sun sets eloquently
I feel the vitality in me renew
The sound of the sea
Against the distant shore

The sensation of ease inner peace to restore
No utterance to assault the senses
No pledged fabrications, only natural truths
Built on solid foundations
Such beautiful resilience
To gradual change
No forceable demands
No self to rearrange
A place where time is effortless
Where I can be alone
Where life makes its way
Like a blade of grass through stone

The Queen of Shell

By Yanny Widjanarko

Evil creeps upon the ceiling of a conscience
Camouflaged as hanging bait she called love
Curiosities and wonders abate for a jealousy
Intrigues had woven from the length of her string
Incubated ambitions, hatched her spectrums
Creating the realm of her own perfections
Where slums, the place she lives, her jail
And synthetic life is the rail to pass her dreams
Comparison is the bible of her wisdom
Where omission had never been written
Inking her throne in the bias of her ripple
Until the day she found, the defect speaks
Her paradise has fallen
The glitch of the past is hazing
Haywiring her next OCD plans
Living with the leftover of the failures
It is her world collapsed by vanity
Yet, darkness owns her
She roams the uncertainty
Spare her logic to the blanket of selfishness
With half of her leg, she walks
Exploring the impurity.

Into the Unknown

By Jesse Batista

So long I've believed an eternity of despair
would be my resultant path
Isolation in a world I have come to distrust
A belief that I must walk alone
What now
Another soul left to feel the pain
Stranded and confused
I feel a kindred spirit has infiltrated my heart
Understanding of the shadows left behind
Of the torments still to come
Like two roses on a single stem
Our roots intertwine, grounding us
We stand stronger than one
The road ahead blurred and uncertain
We can withstand the unforeseen
Each relying on the other to ease the burden
To take solace in the storms
Where we were once pelted by the falling rain
now seems a light mist
Shall we dance in the wind to the tune of the thunderous booms
Let the flashes of intense light lead us into the unknown
Trust now defined in measures of hope
Let the anguish wash away
Take my hand and let us walk into obscurity together

Depression

By Rob Bristol

Cannot seem get to sleep, waking through the night,
Recurring nightmares which you try to fight,
No one pays attention when you're in a mood,
You lose your sense of appetite when preparing food.

Opting for the solitude, remaining home alone,
Counting all the tears, whilst being on your own,

Feeling down and useless, a burden to your friends,
Trapped within a vortex, with no happy ends.

Crying out inside you, torment of the mind,
Missing family members you chose to leave behind,
Forever on the telephone to hear a friendly voice,
Hiding in the darkness appears your only choice.

Seeking for a reason for you to carry on,
Believing none shall miss you when you're dead and gone,
Haunted by the shadows which make up your past,
Holding fate responsible for the problems it has cast.

You lose your sense of appetite when preparing food,
Flying off the handle when you are in a mood,
Waiting for the nightmares to keep your mind awake,
Depriving you a good night's sleep, despite the pills you take...

The Night Vision

By Kristina Bray

At night I dream of my dear love. By heaven she is fair!
I see her lying on my bed, enrobed in golden hair,
Her pale hand curved beneath her cheek as she smiled wistfully.
Would it be wrong, think you, to hope somewhere
she thinks of me?
Her skin is pink as a conch shell. Her smooth,
white cheeks are flushed.
There is a music in her breath that ennobles night's hush.
Her every curve and limb is formed in perfect symmetry.
How could a poor man merit the sight of such rare beauty?
I cannot say, but her dear vision keeps nightmares away.
She defends me from all peril, shining 'til break of day.
Though she has travelled far away to a much better place
And I cannot call myself hers, yet I hold to her grace.
Does her image not break my heart? Indeed, the pain bites through.
I was not good enough for her but yet I cannot rue
The hours I spent holding her as she dreamed next to me.
Another watches her dream now, but she's a part of me.

Life's Rhythms and Rhymes

By Diane LabonGray

Throughout time we twist our rhythm and rhymes,
Like fine wine,
Spilling throughout time,
Dancing on our hearts and minds,
Like a distant drum,
Echoing on the wind,
To the heart beat,
Like sweet wine,
Flowing through our lost minds,
As the painting on the wall,
Tells the story for us all,
As the silhouettes of sand,
Play in the band,
Like the violin,
Signing in the wind,
As hearts are broken again and again,
As the darkness comes,
Then goes,
We all grow cold,
And the dance of life goes around and around,
Like a marry go around,
Till you feel like a lost clown,
As the Rhythm of the street,
That's at your feet,
Keeps calling,
As the children of the night,
Can't stop crying into the lonely cold night,
As the Rhythm of time dances,
And as one door is opened,
Another is closed,
And locked
As the silhouettes that are left,
Are like paint running down the wall,
And the music that is played in the park,
Just numbs our hearts,
As life ends and starts,
We lose our way,

Even by the light of day,
Mankind forgets to pray,
And just wants to play,
As the violin plays a soft and sweet melody,
A melancholy lullaby,
As our children die high,
We learn to say goodbye,
But can't cry,
As time ticks on and on,
The dancing and romancing,
And wine and song goes on,
As one door opens to another day,
And the drummer is found dead,
Without a home or bed,
And the poet's words,
Are so bittersweet,
As they echo throughout time,
Lost in a twisted nursery rhyme,
As the pages of time are torn out of man's holy book,
And rolled up and smoked,
And another child is lost to crack or coke,
Or is found at the end of a rope,
Are we so blind to the times,
Or can you still feel the wind blow,
And see out your window of your soul,
Or has your heart gone cold.

Fetching Water

By Joe Callanan

The grass will grow
down in the meadow,
if the sun shines strong,
it will grow long.
I'll open a route,
with dirtied boot,
walking to the well,
upon the Angelus bell.

I'll carry the water,
in open pitcher,
I'll quietly whisper,
changing hands,
stopping too,
more than once,
certainly a few,
then I'll stand.

In a leafy place,
my breath will
take in the space,
of my standing still,
near an apple tree.
welcoming me...
as a timeless thrill,
shares its face.

My heart shivers,
trembled as it caught,
the whole lot
of its timeless whispers,

all that survives still,
of open space,
and freedom's will,
still moving stirs.

Walk on Bye

By Diane LabonGray

Living on the bye and bye
with the children of the night
Watching the people just walk on by,
Should I cry when it's cold outside,
without anything to eat accept
the trash from the streets,

or shoes on my cold feet,
As I see the lonely people
like you and me,
Just walk on bye,
Living and dying,
On the bye and bye,
We are born in this free land,
But I ask God what was his plans
As I see the rich and poor,
Just walk on by,
But not knowing why,
Crying about life
or the chill in the air tonight,
Want put a penny in my cup,
Nor worm my bones,
So Dear Lord if you're out tonight,
And walking by,
Lord just take me home,
where I can't feel the cold in my bones,
Nor the hunger in my soul,
Here in this free land,
Living and dying with
the children of the night,
Oh please lord if I die tonight,
Don't just walk on bye.
Let me lay by your feet at your fireside,
And serve you one last time.

The World Doesn't Care About Poetry

By Rafik Romdhani

Why doesn't the world care about poetry
while all eyes are dripping with dark images
distilled from hearts that have been crushed
by hardships and sad nights?
Only a few carry the burden of this boring universe,
Only a few turn tears
into a torrent of expressive words.

Why doesn't a poet appear on TV
and recite his poems to children
so that they understand that the night
is a door into distant imagination?
Why are poems not sold at the Chemists
like medicine and I would receive them
from a lady's eyes, the colour of my dream?
Why won't you let the poetic flow take my fever
in its direction to the sanctuary of the soul?
This world has no listening ears
It just throws the bard into the dungeon
of oblivion where he might be seen
as a joke in the form of a phantom
who speaks the words of wizards and fools.
Why do you only see bodies in bodies
and disagree that poetry is the material
from which the air we breathe was created.
Where else aside from art could you find truth?
Where else would words live in peace?
This body containing me was only a heartbeat,
a fabric brimming with all that is recondite.
Sounds are the origin which builds the tangible
and solid things around us.
So, why don't you let poetry rebuild the rubble
you used to worship with verve?

Waiting for Rebirth

By P. L. Minx

So tired of being the glue,
watching it all unravel,
broken pieces,
stuck,
raining down all at once.
I can't be your everything:
Ms. Independent
Ms. Strong
Ms. Satisfy-you-all-night-long.
Where's my satisfaction?

Where's my joy?
Am I just
Some toy to dispose of,
treat like rotting garbage,
complaining the odor
stings your nose?
The scent of dread,
moments away
from death,
flashes of what could have been…
Slow dances in the kitchen,
spontaneous kisses,
wild nights on the beach
watching waves splash at our feet,
beaming with adoration
at me in my little black dress
holding me so tenderly
in times of distress.
Yet,
Years were wasted
yearning for the impossible;
Watching you,
watching me,
in disgust,
never being good enough,

wondering my worth,
praying for rebirth.
Stumbling through life,
panting in pain,
screaming for solace,
but nobody came.
So I lick these tears,
salty and grey,
waiting and wanting,
praying for rain,
To nurture,
To love,
To live
Once again.

The Fireside Chair

By Amanda Wilson

An empty chair by the fireside bare,
the hearth offers no succour, no warmth felt.
Fire untended, un-stoked, unprepared,
this house a warm home when 'twas here you dwelt,
an air of loneliness leaves all heartfelt.
To the chair I'll talk, as it does to me,
your presence sensed but I cannot see.

Focused thoughts midst the smouldering ember
where once did glow many a hearthstone flame.
Ashes ne'er cold but warm hearts remember,
memories steadfast, glowing all the same.
Never forgotten, I will call your name.
Senses despair unable to find home,
both feeling lost and we both feel alone.

A mantle photo, memories of you,
ruminating so and much to regard.
Devoid of content the chair grieved to view
In wake of your loss our family marred.
A face of wellbeing; just a façade.
An honour that's mine you've made me the heir
of your loved and treasured fireside chair.

Rise, Butterfly

By Antonella Caiazza

As I watched in horror,
or read every new tweet
of the bodies dropping
all around me,
A part of me died.
Some days, I died 1000 times...
We tried our best to keep moving.
Live our lives day by day,

But the fear just gnawed and gnawed,
and the anger chipped away,
at the lives we created,
as we realized we were dead,
Long ago,
Buried,
but still (barely) breathing.
The screams became deafening.
We bargained but felt cheated.
The sadness drowned us, slowly.
Resentment left us so defeated.
Will we accept this as our fate?
Is this life worth living for?
Is there hope for new beginnings?
Should we give up and start over?
We've had so much time to think
of the meaning of our lives.
We've spent day after day
wondering if we would survive.
I'm done thinking.
I'm done fearing.
I'm done giving.
I'm done losing.
I just want to be living.

Tired of feeling unfulfilled
while days and years pass us by.
There must be more to life
and I want more before I die.

So I'm working on self-love
And resurrecting pieces of me,
Parts I lost slowly through the years,
chunks of soul bitten by scrutiny.
As I transform, wounds heal.
Laughter and lyrics make my soul thrive.
And I rise, break free of the cocoon.
I fly freely.
I survive.

Walking in the Rain

By Naomi G. Tangonan

coming out at dawn
for a morning walk
the sky cloudy but the
quarter moon shines
brightly
i pass by rice fields
and mahogany trees
birds chattering endlessly
morning mist is cold but the
breeze is gently soothing
soon i hear the pitter patter
of rain on crisp dry leaves
by the roadside getting louder
and bolder, clouds turn to grey
and the moon hides from view
i hurry and run to go
back home or i'll be soaking wet
but while it rained there was that
dreamy moment in walking-running
against the rain like chasing a dream
in some faraway place
why be afraid of the rain
never mind getting wet
it's a beautiful feeling
let me enjoy the raindrops
on my hair, on my face,
on my tongue, embracing

my whole being
then my spirit becomes alive
i've become friends with the rain
and enjoy its intimate company
like an old familiar friend
so eagerly welcomed
all is well i whistle
a happy tune
home at last.

Sitting by the Thames under Overcast Skies

By David Arndt

Sitting by the Thames under overcast skies
Life has changed
In ways I don't understand why
Old life sheds its skin
In the wind new songs sing
Songs letting go of yesterday's sorrow
Songs not fearing what will be tomorrow
Songs arising from earth a flower
Songs healing restoring life's power
Heart opens more with each passing hour
Suffering of before
Clouds
Slowly float by
Dissipating
In overcast
London skies
Hearts purpose
No longer ignored
Nor denied
By the Thames river
Mourning
The one I loved before
Only you found a way to unlock
My lonely heart's door
I say farewell love
Watching a rusted barge pass by
So many years
Seems like yesterday
I throw your ashes
Watch them blow in the breeze
Become one with the river
Which flows to the sea
I Let you go
Stepping
Into life

Anew
Leaving
You
Behind
Sitting
By the
Thames
Under
Overcast
Skies

The Fragrance of Remembering

By Marie Harris

The familiar fragrance
Of daddy's cigar
Comes wafting through my memories
As if from a magic jar

A picture of him comes to mind
In his big old comfy rocker
Sitting, listening to the quiet as he was want to do
Waiting patiently for his warm peach cobbler

The front porch and the mountain Vista
Saturate my soul with reminiscing
Summer breeze through the trees
And a yearning for more than just remembering

Once in a while he would tell a story
From his well-worn memory book
A delight while the crickets sang
Listening to the rolling gentle melody
from a passing brook

Gone is the front porch
Gone is his fragrant cigar
Gone with only memories

Another Place, Another Time

(For those we've lost)

By Neil Forsyth

Every drop of rain
That falls from a darkened sky,
Is a tear that cascades,
From my hollowed eyes.
Every cloud that forms,
Every shade of grey,
Reminds me of when
You passed away.

Every ship that sails,
To a distant sea,
To a different sunset,
I know you'll be.
From the pain you suffered,
To fatality,
From a world of hurt,
To one that's pain free.

Every dream I've had,
Every dream come true,
Is one that's wished,
In memory of you.
Every grandchild's laughter,
Every smile, every frown,
Reminds me of when
You were still around.

But time has elapsed,
Now you have moved on,
Every time I wonder,
Why have you gone?

Mavis Cane

By David Arndt

Mavis Cane
Going nowhere in the fast lane
Pushes on despite the pain
How she does it I can't explain
Life for Mavis is a runaway train

Barely meets the rent or eats
She's not far from living on the streets

Working three jobs a day
No time to get away
On a conveyor belt
Melt melt melt
Normalized reality
Blinding Humanity
Suffering indignities

Mavis Cane has seen it all
She took a fall but still stands tall
She has no fear
Pushes away her tears

Despite living a life with endless strife
She is grateful to have a precious life

Mavis has it tough
It's rough
Bills she can't pay
So beaten down
Her minds in a haze
Mavis Cane
Her life's insane
Runaway train
But she carries on
She is strong
Inspires me
To face reality
Abide and be

My dear friends let's wake up
Haven't we had enough
Violence and greed
Corrupted seed
Division growing like weeds?

Can't you see
Things are broke
We're in a
Death spiral choke
Skeleton hands

Grip our throats

Let's wake up and be real
Let's learn how to feel
It's possible to care
It's possible to be aware

Let's build bridges of compassion
Love and compassion never go out of fashion

These stars can guide our way
These dark times can pass away
There is a chance for humanity
We need to shift to the slow lane
All this out of control technology
Is blowing up our brains
Humanities good qualities
Are going down the drain
What we call progress
Causes destruction and pain
Isn't this obvious
It's as clear as a window pane
Do I need to explain?
Why are we flushing ourselves
Down the drain?

Mavis Cane I'm so grateful to you
I know it you can make it we can make it too

We can rise above.
We'll rise Above with love

Soaring, like a dove

Beneath peaceful Skies.
Can you see this truth
Reflected in my eyes?
Can we start over and try?

We can I swear it's possible
But we must act now for love and life
If not the changes will be irreversible
I will stop here but ask all of you
Do these words ring true?

Mavis Cane I'm grateful to know you
If you made it we will make it too
You faced your hell
The tolling of the bells
Came out the other side
With so much love inside
Just like you Mavis
We will make it through
I know this to be true

Downside Up

By Mel Broughton

'Twas busy in the still of night
You could hear the roaring quiet
Two tiny cats and a giant mouse
Had a silent riot.

I was quite perturbed with peace of mind
And so I lay down to stand
To figure out what was going on
And slipped my shoes upon my hand.

Feeling wide asleep, I skipped upstairs,
But I grinned my biggest frown.
I soon realised what I had done:
I'd put the day on upside down!

Villanelle for an Acorn

By Adam Whitworth

It's not what you should do, it's what you can
creating more than giving and taking
my love saved my heart from her tired divan

All the world in an unmoved caravan
making room for love the undertaking
It's not what you should do, it's what you can

So far had I wandered a lone woodsman
as evening fell I heard a sweet singing
my love saved my heart from her tired divan

I had no rose and no wit for a plan
so doubled her wood-pile, axe a-swinging
It's not what you should do, it's what you can

She opened her door, held a frying pan
laughing and eating, not dancing, prancing
my love took my heart to her tired divan

Oh acorn, from which our shady woods began
ever and ever I'm praising, thanking
It's not what you should do, it's what you can
my love saved my heart from her tired divan

Mother of Moths

By C.L. Liedekev

My mother
is born of the sorry
he left on the voicemail,
the flap of missing months,
born of couches on fire.
The house of gasoline
finds its queen with her mouth

slack as moth wings.
My mother
is the forgiveness
of shovels and workmen,
of screams as the DTs
piss out of veins and eyes.
His venom as relapse, as the scales
grow across the doorframe.
She will summon sleep, night
time tour after tour in flames, melting
her love into plastic animal scars.
My mother
writes these mistakes in soot,
in her daughter's name molded
by shame-chanted urges,
prayer spelled in biker-speak means wound.
For her, memory becomes the war,
tongues become the weapons
of her sharp and exhausted mornings.
She smokes in the darkness,
the message climbing to char-stain
the ceiling and gone.
The rise and slur of his voice
breaks her apart each time.
Each time she is born again
in the bright dust falling into carpet.

Poetry and Me

By Amanda Wilson

At night I'm hard hit, at three maybe four,
a brain unrestrained, words left to run free,
outlined collections, poetry in store,
unorganised notes and penning for me.
I gather thoughts, await my morning coffee.
Villanelles, pentameters, half done odes,
every style imagined, every mode.

I'm a poet with concepts varying,

eclecticism and stanzas diverse,
poems appealing each page revealing
the 'sublime and ridiculous' in verse.
Some a narrative and some rather terse.
Mystic images created from word,
meant to be written and meant to be heard.

Succinct of word, visuals are distinct,
image poetic from a turn of phrase,
oration, delineation penned with ink,
narration, illustration bygone days.
Oft I'm critical, my own work I rephrase.
Pencraft enjoyment, not looking for praise.
Romantic, fantastic, thoughts, notes and cues
which style of poem would you now pursue?

A poem preference is different for all
a stanza read and a page turned swiftly,
some too traditional some off the wall
context convey, courteous in poetry.
Each verselet to read, has sincerity.
A poet's work is filled with emotion,
It's feelings, thoughts, it's their composition.

Voice

By Vincent Blaison

Crowded misconceptions in an empty room
Drowning in silence
As the voices of fear attempt to deter my progression
Breathe...
Calm the mind
So the heart may sing
Push past myself
So my spirit can flow
Mending the wounds from the fall
So the true self may spring forth

Each step upon the water
Sends ripples only viewed upon the surface
Yet, piercing every direction
Through the depths
And into the Heavens
"Find your voice....."
"V o i c e"
"v o i c e..."
As the echo dissipates into the distance
It is time,
Destiny has arrived.

Autumn Reverie

By Marie Harris

Autumn memories curl around
Shimmering, dancing in her reverie
Passing like quicksilver draining
Through the sieve of her memory

Falling slowly, softly floating
their beauty resting
Tiny shadows of yesterday
In the corner of her mind waiting

Her introspective meandering
Through the seasons changing
Gather momentum in the fall
When her life was suddenly rearranging

Tempting is the looking back
To relive moments held in time and space
Melodies playing slightly out of tune
Just well-worn memories to put back in place

Gone are the halcyon days
When life offered love plentiful and sweet
Growing in vines of perpetuity
Found now where love in memory meets

Autumn in its beautiful wonder
A harbinger of memories forthcoming
When love for them was bright and blooming
The melody of their love faithfully strumming

On a beautiful Autumn day
With the leaves falling
A crisp scent of change in the air
The echo of love's goodbye can be heard calling

She will always miss him
And the love they shared
Autumn walks with forever in mind
When tomorrow was just another day
Until death claimed him in the beauty of Autumn's time

Smile on My Face Though

By Shafkat Aziz

Smile on my face though
Dejected is my heart.
I make people happy though
In woes I am caught.
I'm in my bed though
Can't sleep well,
I wake up at dawn
Coz all night I weep.
I feel I am though
I am not what I must be.
I feel I am sighted though
Good things I can't see.
In quest of comfort I'm though
Rapacity beats my heart faster,
Coz it's my worst foe.
O All- hearing, all-seeing and all-knowing
Free my heart from yearnings
For what I need not,
Let me do what I will
This is all I want.

That Cold Winter's Day

By Kirsty Howarth

Silence surrounds me
And I'm all alone
Things left unsaid
If only I'd known
I talk to you
But don't think you hear
So far away
Yet so very near
I remember that day
We were torn apart
It felt like something
Had been ripped from my heart
Now I'm drowning
In the depths of despair
Wondering and hoping
That you still care
The days pass by
It's been so long
But the radio still plays
Our favourite song
Everything is bleak
And cold and grey
Still connected to you
But worlds away
The snow still falls
The wind still blows
The world keeps turning
Round and round it goes
I no longer cry
We can no longer touch
But I hope you know
I loved you so much
I tried to hold on
Whilst beside you I lay
The day that I died
On that cold winter's day

Blessed

By Joe Callanan

Blessed are the mirrors
Holding back dark reflections
Hiding unseen errors
Of hardened looks
Judgemental deep inspections
In fantasy books
Borrowed from desire of agility
Born out of fragility
To examine a while
Before they spoil

Blessed are the smiles
Peacefully obscuring
The diversity insuring
Of thumbs up in fake trials
On diets where loss of pounds
Is on corporate rounds
On crash collisions of fist pumps
Where only society can stay high
Watching how the piston jumps
In markets hung out to dry

Blessed are the forgotten class
The poor dumb beasts the silly ass
Birds of night birds of day
Birds in flight birds on the prey
Birds chosen to stay
In cages thrown seed
Birds kept out of the way
Unless they suit a need
On a collision course of pigeon chesting
Handshakes with slapping high fives
Even one set apart rarely thrives
On higher intelligence in tried testing

Blessed are the dominoes

Set out neatly in rows
Each situation shows
Backbone zip like spine
Virtual virtues lessons online
Hidden zen of forgotten practice
The refined looks of an ageing actress
Sweetened smiles mirror correct
In daytime robbery no-one is suspect
Each one knowing falls into place
For others arriving face to face

The Passions of Adonis

By Rosario Aurelius

"Is this what I look like?" said the artist, timid and shy,
He had the hosts of London eating from his hand,
coming home to the nightmare of the ancestral land,
He was no witch yet he made a vow to never grow old,
his heart already sold,
He sought love to unite with ideals of virtue and right,
a soft lightness he cast on the sea of watchful eyes,
This Adonis, not til his head turned for pleasure,
his eidolon cured the pain
Of the nightmarish ancestral shame,
yet his story is the tale of every man
whose philosophy was ever attacked,
By the measure of the youthful impact,
as men stand before the crossroads at an impasse,
Longing again for youth while fearing Saturn's leaden sickle,
middle age is ever so fickle,
Fortune's hand has not yet turned man's heads
from the ideal to the surreal,
still a babe he drowns himself in the perfume
of passion to steal,
As the babe learns to feel its way through Plato's cave,
youthful Adonis the object of fawning learns to play cute
To break the glass menagerie of social convention
by grasping at the root
and tearing asunder the veil of illusion that hangs

like the spectre of spectral reality
The audacious and wicked gleam that laughed
in the face of social morality,
the voice that whispered "There are no limits,"
to what the youthful Adonis may acquire,
That he hath every right to seize each desire,
every desire an experience in becoming,
Self-actualized, self-fulfilled, yet every shadow road
leads to mountainous heights and as sinuous depths corrode
Become babe of the abyss to explore
the deepest caverns along the shore,
There Adonis descended into Hell,
where the poison of God and demons of the earth dwell,
Where he dug up the devil to wear his face,
returning to the salons and public space,
Only now the middle aged who once fawned
on young Adonis wept,
and cried in horror as the winds swept
them by, and left Adonis as a sun that never sets
his soft devil face and his eidolon stretched,
His perfumed idol no longer the idyllic youthful Adonis
bless'd, become the worm ridden corpse where all the
shadows rest,
Woven into the dust of death,
and the buzzing sunken chest, rising and falling
with Beelzebel's breath.

Colored Memories

By Jannetta Lamourt

Wildly pink roses—
splattered over my sunshine jacket
as I stood in the glistening snow, toes cold in my
black boots.
My brother begs me not to tell mom he broke
the rule. He hadn't my wisdom at a year older to
know
I would allow him to stew for a while—

but never be so cruel.
The drapery of deep purple—
slathered in swirls and curls of pink and red.
One long night our bedroom hazed with fevered dreams
where snakes slithered in the silence of my fear.
I learned to hide from the monsters outside my bed.
Bunk beds coated with fluorescent orange—
layered thick to cover the raw grain of two-by-fours,
Mom found the color in the discount section
of Simpson's hardware.
The lulling squeak-squeak, squeak-squeak
in rhythmic to and fro
my little brother rocks himself to sleep in the bed below.
Lady Clairol Golden Copper Highlights
mother's hair in permed loop and larrup
She stands still in the early morning light,
her legs snowy against a flowered cotton house dress
an open invitation for a hummingbird to hesitate in a
hungry hover

At the Bus Stop

By Joe Callanan

Standing in the rain,
waiting at the bus stop,
just up from the corner shop.
Overhead circled a plane
already flying low,
ready to descend in Heathrow.

Two girls on their way to school,
stand in front of timetable schedule,
both barely glancing at me.
Pointing to scribbled graffiti,
one said it looked like her fella's tattoo.
The bus was unusually late,
it was getting close to eight,
it was almost twenty to.

Polka dotted with chewing gum,
the footpath welcomed a sweet wrapper,
one slagging her friend, over her bum,
threatened, that for less she'll slap her,
if not careful, she'll land her a right one,
and knock her halfway to Brighton.

A brave sparrow flitted his dance,
between the feet of all of us waiting,
searching for crumbs, took his chance,
in the soft rain now slowly abating.
The girls talked tougher by the minute,
swearing and constantly saying "innit".

The man who lived next door to me,

but, who was never neighbourly,
he saw me, pretending not to see,
now did me an unknowing favour,
crossing the road before a passing car,
my mate called from not too far,
seeing me, as he braked to slow down,
"Hurry up, we are going to town!"

As the Wind Chills them Factory Gates

By Neil Forsyth

They swarm in their droves,
Those nine to fives,
As the snowflakes stick,
It's their working lives.
Uphill they trudge,
Down dales they file,
Sacrificial in bringing up
Wife and Child.
Cold tears through their chests
Each day they endure,

Cold tears drop down
Their faces, impure.
A hard-earned wage,
That don't come with ease,
As this worsening winter,
Becomes a deep- freeze.
Frozen assets won't melt
As each day rolls by,
As workers dig in
With profits sky high.
Factory smoke litters
The clearest sky,
Still seagull and petrel,
On wings they do fly.
A Lancashire setting,
Picturesque and serene,
Of fields turned to white,
Where once verdant green.
Reminiscent of Lowry,
And his Matchstick Men,
Every day these workers
Will trudge on again.

Origin of Anger

By C.L. Liedekev

I toss and turn at night,
smell up the sheets
with late-night bowls
of Lucky Charms. My kids
are asleep and I polish
the memories
of the beer bottle
shattered in my father's shoulder.
The brown glass memory
like a North Star I can't
reach. When I push
out my hand,

it is as tiny again
holding my Charon
action figure with
its coinless face gone grey.
My mother the metal face.
We both invoke
my father's blood
like party streamers
in reverse to the black
gate of my bedroom.
And finally, I'm crying
in a wave of anger
that has a human form.

As We Walk Majestically

By Octobias Obie Mashigo

As we walk majestically
Under blue sky
Fresh breeze easing our minds
Hand in hand exchanging
Romantic poems floating on
Our lips
Sharing sonnets of kisses
Verbally printing footprints
Of our love on clean

Hope my king
We are not too late
To let our hearts skate
On clean slate
To light candles of love
For us again

It's not too late
To delete the past
And start afresh
For us to let love bloom
Again in our hearts

Hearts are clean
More than an empty book
That is ready to rewrite
What we erased day
We let sun sat on us
While anger was still feeding
on us

My queen
It is not too late for us to
Love again
Frame this journey of love
On walls of our hearts
Art in our minds thee future
We want to be featured in
In our journey of love

And forget about thy days
And past that made anger
Deflowered our hearts and minds
Trust that was resting peaceful
In the depths of our hearts

It is too late
To look back and complain
About our mistakes
Let's put the past behind us
Hide tears of years of pain
In our relationship
And let's let love bind us together again

For us to keep on printing
Footprints of our love
On clean slate
For late nights to start lighting
Candles of love for us again
On moonless nights
Without judging mistakes
We made in the past
When past was thine advisor

White Swans and Ice

By Rhiannon Owens

Through frozen dreams I ride a white swan
as necks elegantly arch into feathered hearts,
the embrace of lovers as they become one

and the ice is not cold, I am not numb
I've come alive, sailing into this silvered night,
the sky is flawless onyx, smooth obsidian illuminated
by the purity of the moon and stars,

I have journeyed far
right through the crystalline curtain of ice
now hanging gossamer-like,

A fixed cascade of sparkling perfection
a backdrop to this place where all my dreams came
true...

Thanksgiving

By Yusuf M. Khalid

Within the twinkle of an eye
—a finger snap
I felt like galvanic and high
after a nap
Nothing's band was cut by a knife
—I was present
I was given the rose of life
as a present

Didn't expect such a surprise
I never did
It was free though beyond the price
of highest bid
I want to thank Allah who gave
life as a gift
A brine of thanks with such a wave
sublime and swift

Reach for the Stars

By Deepti Shakya

Get up and stop crying, set your goal,
Spread your wings to climb the highest summit.
Ignite the flame within you to touch the sky,
Your determination will only take you to the destination.

Surely there will be many obstacles in your way,
But you have to overcome those obstacles fearlessly.
Keep your goal in mind and keep moving forward,
You just have to believe in your potential and ability.

Prepare yourself to face every challenge,
No matter what happens, you don't have to give up.
Just chase your dreams and believe in God,
Never let go of your passion.

One day your hard work will definitely pay off,
Never let yourself be weak, be strong.
Surely one day you will reach for the stars,
And you will shine with your brilliant success.

Heavenly Waters

By DeJuan Jamel O'Halloran

From the murky,
shallow estuary
streams,
I walk through
them to be with the
sea.

Submerging myself
in the saltiness, gentle
waves of the warm
waters that surround me.

I swam onward calmly,

towards the coral reefs
deeper into the ocean's
aqua artistry arrays
of colors and patterns.

Ripples,
in the distance
I see dolphins playing
flipping and dipping over
and under rocks,
what a sight to behold.

In no hurry,
no rush
the ocean has nowhere to go,
it can move in miraculous ways
creating immense tides
and waves.

As I gazed into the distance
I saw a multitude of fish
swimming in circular
formations.

Descending further
into uncharted
darkness,
as blue turns to black,
in the unilluminated
indefinite waters.

The pure stillness
that be in the endless
vastness of the
Oceanic sea.

This such an astonishing
surprise,
I could still notice the stars
way up in the skies.

The Cry of the Dying Ferns

By Sinazo Zoe Ngxabani

When we were young and foolish
Full of blindfolded trust
we rolled in the hay on carefree days,
when the rain fell off heaven's
glory, our face lifted up to taste the falling rain
before it was deemed poisonous.

With nothing but the dust on the ground
When all was simple; the trust in our hearts,
not even death could cripple.
Before the cruelty of the grasp of life
Could ever ripple.

Who knew that our daily ways could bring
the forest to an age of wrinkles.
Nature forced to age, summoned by
pollution to a state so fickle.
I long to see the eyes of endangered trees
sear into a twinkle,
choked by smog, suffocating
through the anxiety of death clouds of danger
born out of the womb of pollution protocol
violations.

Oil is wealth to hell with health,
while corporations drown themselves in quadrillions
the screams of babies born with deformities
breathing the air of smoking—choking death weaved by
careless unscrupulous money hungry wolves in suits.

Ban the plastic that made its way to the cow's throat.
Ban the burning of waste that ascends its flames
and fumes fuelled by the fury of the future into
the clouds—my pathway to heaven.

Tuberculosis wars and airborne diseases
Summoned by sunless days ahead,

The air is as unclean
as the demonic spirit of child slavery
and human trafficking—no not in the
nineteenth century right now today,
God please hear me pray, make a way.

Listen to the pleas of the dying forest
awaiting for a recitation;
The ferns of the forests are breathing
through their wounds
and no one is reasoning only a few
are trying to save the last dancing ferns,
still not many are listening or at least aiding.

The cry of the ferns is choked by the capitalism
of the morally decayed man in a Balenciaga
attire who cleans his conscience by driving a car
which he claims is environmentally friendly.
Are you listening?
Society gives him a pass and calls him
a noble hero of environmental friendliness;
A reward for killing life in its entirety—
This is our reality.

Yet in the meantime the cry of the dying ferns
is unheard better yet a scream ignored.
Are you listening to the cry of the dying ferns
moved by gales for comfort, showered by acid rain
for more discomfort?
Are you listening to the cry of the ferns
and inkwood trees as the palm trees await a storm from
the rain of nuclear bombs in the atmosphere?

Listen to the cry of the world,
Listen to the cry of mother nature,
Listen to the cry of the dying ferns.

Outside Your Window

By S. D. Kilmer

Outside your window
I stand.
Beneath the tree.
There you might not see.

Me here thinking and wondering
How you are.
And how you pass the time.
It's unbelievable you were once mine.

I wonder where you are.
And if you still sing our song.
How you live the days so long.
Where did we go wrong?

I walked left at the intersection.
You walked straight ahead.
I suppose this is the reason.
We could never live through the seasons.

I hope you are well,
As well as I.
When you think of us
Please do not cry.

our way home

By Matthew Elmore

I wrote this poem and called it a song
just for you to sing along
blazing trails I longed to claim
until a day that I am finally gone
proven right from being so wrong

what is beauty but truth adorned
I've written so many, many poems
decorated with fancy words and plain
both together and alone
you and I shared these lines as one

we both celebrated and mourned
sometimes two times three times scorned
starting so different ended up some same
pricked and bled from the same thorn
roamed alone then found our way home

we both admired the coming storm
conquered joy over being forlorn
celebrated a life and gave her a name
I wrote this poem and called it a song
just for you to sing along

Ashes in the Wind

By Brandon Adam Haven

Hovering o'er the decayed straw beset
Shadowing a mountainous hill on the terrain
Thunder loudly roars, the ground becomes wet
As lightning crashes loud enough
to wake even the dead
A mortal sin, undefined holding
an intense rage inside
Bludgeoning wearily my conscience within
I ponder forth scattering her ashes in the wind

I feel deep in my soul
dreadful wrath uncontrolled
Forbidding thoughts, deep
into the Stygian of ire.
Eyes of fire, mortality expired
Plummeting into the perception
of hallucination excelled
I tremble yet am quell,
gentle anguish foretells

Amid the trench of the valley basin
Flooded and desolate, loudly atoned
Withering anew, chastise emotions grown
Scattering deep into the humid mournful dew
My love now free from her skin,
the torn-fullness within
In wet pilgrimage I lay embracing her fate
But still feeling intense vexation within
I ponder forth scattering her ashes deep
into the loud stormy wind

WHEELSONG POETRY ANTHOLOGY

About Wheelsong Books

Wheelsong Books is an independent poetry publishing company
based in the ocean city of Plymouth,
on the beautiful Southwest coast of England.
Established by poet Steve Wheeler in 2019,
the company aims to promote previously unheard voices
and encourage new talent in poetry. Wheelsong is also
the home of the Absolutely Poetry anthology series,
featuring previously unpublished and emerging poets
from around the globe.

Wheelsong has more poetry publications in the pipeline!
You can read more about Wheelsong Books and its growing stable
of exciting new and emerging poets on the
Wheelsong Books website at: wheelsong.co.uk

Wheelsong publication list

- Ellipsis (2020) by Steve Wheeler
- Inspirations (2020) by Kenneth Wheeler
- Sacred (2020) by Steve Wheeler
- Living by Faith (2020) by Kenneth Wheeler
- Urban Voices (2020) by Steve Wheeler
- Small Lights Burning (2021) by Steve Wheeler
- My Little Eye (2021) by Steve Wheeler
- Ascent (2021) by Steve Wheeler
- Dance of the Metaphors (2021) by Rafik Romdhani
- Into the Grey (2021) by Brandon Adam Haven
- RITE (2021) by Steve Wheeler
- Absolutely Poetry Anthology 1 (2021) by various
- Absolutely Poetry Anthology 2 (2022) by various
- War Child (2022) by Steve Wheeler
- Hoyden's Trove (2022) by Jane Newberry
- Shocks and Stares (2022) by Steve Wheeler
- Autumn Shedding (2022) by Christian Ryan Pike
- Cobalt Skies (2022) by Charlene Phare
- Wheelsong Poetry Anthology 1 (2022) by various
- Rough Roads (2022) by Rafik Romdhani

Coming soon…

- Beneath the Surface (2022) by Charlene Phare
- Symphoniya de Toska (2023) by Marten Hoyle

All titles are available for purchase in paperback, and Kindle editions and some in hardcover on Amazon.com or direct from the publisher at: wheelsong.co.uk

Printed in Great Britain
by Amazon

87537985R00102